25 MOUNTAIN BIKE TOURS
in the Adirondacks

Marcy Fields: The Adirondack High Peaks Area

25
MOUNTAIN BIKE
TOURS
in the Adirondacks

Peter Kick

Backcountry Publications
Woodstock · Vermont

An invitation to the reader

Over time, trails and regulations on trail use can and do change, and we invite you to help us keep our guides as up-to-date as possible. If you find changes that have occurred on these routes, please let the author and publisher know, so that corrections may be made in future printings. Other comments and suggestions are also welcome. Address all correspondence to:

Editor, 25 Bicycle Tours Series
Backcountry Publications
P.O. Box 748
Woodstock, Vermont 05091-0748

Library of Congress Cataloging-in-Publication Data

Kick, Peter
   25 Mountain bike tours in the Adirondacks / by Peter Kick. — 1st ed.
      p.   cm.
   ISBN 0-88150-409-2 (alk. paper)
   1. All terrain cycling—New York (State)—Adirondack Mountains—Guidebooks.
2. Bicycle trails—New York (State)—Adirondack Mountains—Guidebooks.
3. Adirondack Mountains (N.Y.)—Guidebooks. I. Title.
GV1045.5.N72A355 1999
917.47'50443—dc21   98-42282
                                                                           CIP

Text and cover design by Sally Sherman
Interior photos by the author, unless otherwise noted
Maps by Henry Christopher, © 1999 The Countryman Press, Inc.
Published by Backcountry Publications
A division of The Countryman Press
P.O. Box 748, Woodstock, VT 05091

Distributed by W. W. Norton & Company, Inc.
500 Fifth Avenue, New York, NY 10110

Printed in the United States of America

10 9 8 7 6 5 4 3 2 1

For June

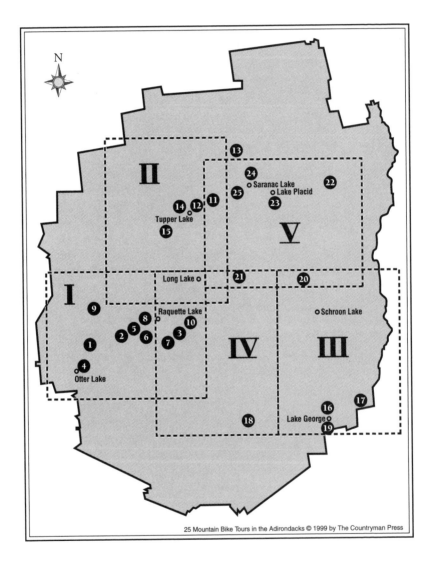

N

II

V

13

24
Saranac Lake
25
Lake Placid
23
22

14 12 11
Tupper Lake
15

I

9

Long Lake

21

20

8
Raquette Lake
5
2 6
1

10
7 3

4
Otter Lake

IV

Schroon Lake

III

18

16
Lake George
19

17

25 Mountain Bike Tours in the Adirondacks © 1999 by The Countryman Press

Contents

Acknowledgments

I would like to thank Richard Fenton, Supervising Forester, New York State Department of Environmental Conservation Bureau of Public Lands, for carefully reviewing the manuscript prior to publication and for providing interpretation, unit management plans, and philosophical input. Thanks are also due to section heads James Papero, Patrick Whalen, and Tad Norton, for reviewing the manuscript.

I would like to recognize Eldon Housinger, the original pioneer of bicycle touring in the Adirondack Park, who by his enthusiasm for bicycling got me started in road touring at a time when there were no existing publications on the subject. He authored *North Country Bike Routes,* which is now out of print, but can be found in most libraries.

Thanks also to Bruce Breitmeyer, manager, and Dave Coulman, consultant, Charles Lathrop Pack Demonstration Forest, SUNY College of Environmental Science and Forestry, for on-site information; and Gary Lee, NYS forest ranger, Moose River Recreation Area, as well as all of the people from the Lands and Forests Bureau who gave me input of any kind; Ted Christodaro, of Pedals and Petals Bike Shop in Inlet, for route-finding and trail information; Gary Filipelli of FlipFlop Bicycle Shop in Lake George for same; the employees and owners of all the Adirondack bike shops, too numerous to name, who showed enthusiasm for this endeavor; and Assistant Forest Ranger Keith Hollenbeck for information about the William C. Whitney Area. Thanks also to Anne O'Dell, author of *Ride New York: 35 Horse and Multiple-Use Trails in the Empire State;* and Elizabeth Folwell, editor of *Adirondack Life* magazine. Thanks also go to my wife, June, for superior endurance, my son, Ryan, for hanging in there, and my sometime riding partner Tim Gifford. Thanks also to the staff at Backcountry Publications: Helen Whybrow for her continuous patience (and extensions); Cristen Brooks for producing the maps; and in particular to the editor of this series, Ann Kraybill.

Stopping by the Bog River on the way to Horseshoe Lake

Introduction

My downstate friends tell me, "The Adirondacks are hard to ride!" Then they show rainbow-colored bruises, maybe some scars and choice scabs, and recount stories about rocks, bogs, blowdowns, mud, bugs, rain, steep trails, endless trails, no trails, and so on. While there is no way to argue with this statement, there are many ways to insure that you personally don't get messed up in this kind of nasty Adirondack terrain, which isn't especially kind to mountain bikers.

If you've ever ridden in the Adirondacks, you'll know the kind of terrain I'm referring to: where you're portaging your bike for hundreds of yards at a time, craving a clear track—or any track—while flesh-chewing blackflies suck at your inner thighs and pry their way under your Lycra, hiding under the protection of your helmet and straps, where they feast on the soft skin behind your ears. Where you've finally given up trying to keep your feet dry and are now wading through streams and muck up to your knees, hoisting your bike just high enough to keep the bottom bracket above the waterline. And where your urge to explore the deep woods—overambitious to begin with—now has you in a near panic to get out in the daylight because you didn't want to carry your headlamp, you've run out of energy bars and gelpaks, and you can't drink the standing water you see and crave so badly since you didn't bring a filter. Meanwhile, you've got friends who are seriously wondering what happened to you and who are at this moment debating whom to call.

These are the kind of situations that anyone who pursues mountain biking with fervor will ultimately encounter—they're just worse in the Adirondacks. But these moments can be minimized with some advance planning, and that's where this book comes in. There's plenty of good trail in the park, and the purpose of this book is to help you weed out the good and the bad from the very, very ugly, so you can enjoy the very best the terrain has to offer.

11

Wild Forest Only, Please!

The Adirondack Forest Preserve—public lands within the Adirondack Park, which contains both state and private land—is administered and protected by the New York State Department of Environmental Conservation (DEC). When the New York State Legislature delegated control of the Adirondack Forest Preserve to the DEC, it also gave them the authority to develop rules and regulations for the management and protection of these lands. Regulations for bicycle use, as for other forest preserve regulations, follow general guidelines as set forth in the Adirondack Park State Land Master Plan, which was originally drafted by the Adirondack Park Agency. Management concerns for the use of ATBs (all-terrain bicycles) on forest preserve lands included issues of safety—for cyclists as well as other groups using the trails—and environmental impact (trail erosion).

Since November 1987, regulations prescribed by the Adirondack Park State Master Plan have prohibited bicycle use in wilderness, primitive, and canoe areas. In both primitive and canoe areas, bikes are prohibited except on those roads designated through the unit management plan process, in which case they will be marked. At this writing, there are no such roads open in these areas, but it is anticipated by the DEC that some will be opened in the future. The total area of primitive lands in the park is between 60–70,000 acres, while there are only about 20,000 acres in the St. Regis Canoe Area (presently the park's only "classified" canoe area). The banning of bicycles to wilderness classified lands has to do with the DEC's sense that mechanized transport is incompatible with wilderness, and that allowing bikes would increase access to interior areas, leading to overuse.

I personally feel that the existing access policy and available space for mountain bikers in the Adirondack Park is both generous and adequate. Unit management plans are being updated to allow for appropriate and continuing ATB use. However, many cyclists feel that the policy is limited and in some ways discriminatory against them (mountain bikers will never be happy). No roads in wilderness areas are open to vehicles except for emergencies such as forest fires and searches, and many advocates of backcountry cycling feel that such roads could be used without causing any damage or user conflicts. Many of these roads are in prime wilderness areas that are currently off-limits to ATBs. It is not entirely out of the question that such areas will be made legal to bicycles in the future, but it won't happen without proactive involvement by the biking public.

All user groups need to think carefully about this. Wilderness areas are defined as those where "the earth and its community of life are untrammeled by man—where man himself is a visitor who does not remain." As an avid hiker and backpacker, I would like to see wilderness kept as wild as possible, which to me does not allow for the presence of bicycles. For what it's worth, I feel the same way about horses. However, horses were not disallowed from wilderness areas because they were thought to be harmless. They were considered a traditional and established presence in the forest preserve at the time the master plan was adopted. Essentially, they were grandfathered in. Horses require a significantly wider and higher travel corridor than bikes do, and their contact material is a steel or aluminum shoe, not just a rubber tire. I have the somewhat old-fashioned view, perhaps, that wilderness should be attained, and is essentially "felt," as a result of arriving under one's own power. I have experienced the irony of these regulations after hiking in 10 miles to relax at a lean-to, only to have a dozen people arrive on horseback, empty their panniers, and set up a small village. But I like horses and horse people. And they are up against the same access challenges that mountain bikers face, only they have even less suitable space to ride in than we do. Remember that you'll be sharing many trails with equestrians. Dismount when they approach, in accordance with IMBA guidelines; they'll thank you for it.

So don't expect every trail in these less-fragile wild-forest areas to be open to bikes. They are evaluated individually, taking into consideration such things as trail conditions, slope, the ensurance of minimal environmental impact, and potential conflicts with other users. There is also no reason for thinking that wild forest lands are any less fragile than wilderness, although that is generally true for higher elevations. Classifications of preserve lands have more to do with contiguous land ownership (especially in the case of wilderness areas) and geographic distribution.

Biking in the Adirondack Park
This book is designed to reflect, support, and promote the growing interest in mountain biking in the Adirondacks. Trails that have been recommended by shops, clubs, and the DEC are described here. Trails that

have not been completed (unlike some other forest preserves, the Adirondacks have no trails designed strictly for all-terrain bikes), and those that aren't well designed or designated for mountain biking—even though in some cases they may be legal—are not included.

Personally, I love riding on dirt roads, but I'm the type of rider who enjoys riding anywhere. It just happens that the Adirondacks have so many scenic dirt roads that it was inevitable that I would include several of them here. Dyed-in-the-wool singletrack riders may take exception, but I believe that once you ride a few of these roads, you'll see why they're irresistible.

Unlike many smaller forest areas in the northeast (such as the Catskills, the Berkshires, the Shawangunks, and the Kittatinnys) the Adirondacks contain nearly 6 million acres and include thousands of miles of legal bike trails and dirt roads. Because of this daunting open space, recreation tends to be most conveniently centered around the tourist towns and state campgrounds that provide controlled access and signed trails, backed up by handouts with maps. I have tried to point out as many of these areas as possible to use as staging grounds, both for the trails in this book as well as for the many others you'll discover.

I've tried to give a genuine feel for the area based on my own experience and sense of satisfaction or dissatisfaction with it, and I will point out opportunities for advocacy where they arise. I have not included trails that I feel are too sensitive or otherwise inappropriate for the kind of sustained use that a guidebook promises. The state lacks the human and financial resources to evaluate trails on an individual basis, or to respond to changing use patterns in a timely manner; therefore we are each personally accountable for some level of responsible stewardship and for determining what should be ridden and what should not, regardless of whether it is legal. The fact that a trail is legal should not be interpreted as carte blanche to ride over anything—and this is why I have chosen not to use any existing, legal, publicized trails that I feel can't retain their present character with sustained pressure by ATBs. The state has been fairly permissive in trail designation, assuming that the less suitable trails with steep slopes, rocks, mud, and roots, would be self-limiting in terms of riding intensity. Specifically, I'm talking about the creation of user patterns that would condemn a trail to a character quite unlike its original condition. This would be unfair to both the landscape and the

Raquette Lake along the Uncas Tour

people who support and maintain it—New York State DEC staff, volunteer trail crews, and taxpayers. I feel that trails should only be designated for bike use if their present condition will not be substantially or irreparably altered by such use.

The Role of Guidebooks

It is my feeling that people do not use guidebooks either as authors and publishers would like them to or expect that they do: carry the books on their person, consult them frequently on the trail in the midst of bugs and deluges, reflect on the commentary. The guidebook-assisted cyclist is not coming to the woods "fresh"—as they would for a personal, first-time discovery—but as a second or hundredth or thousandth visitor to a place, with all of the heaped-up standard responses and interpretations other well-meaning authorities have already offered (each one sounding like the next and few offering anything beyond typical, accepted reactions and responses based on our accepted and often stock relationships to the wilderness). I have tried to keep that in mind by suggesting other areas for exploration and avoiding an unrealistic, omniscient presence as your guide. I feel that we come to the woods to avoid just these same sorts of routines and rat-race postures that we are faced with as programmed individuals in the everyday world—only to find that a bunch of nice publications tell you to go where everyone else is going to do what everyone else is doing.

Instead, I think that people purchase guidebooks as personal inventories of special places, little pieces of the outback that they would like to save for future reference, and then they read about it in the armchair or at the trailhead—and leave it behind. It is my sense that mountain bikers are not the armchair public, however; they would rather ride than read about their subject, and a book is more of a jumping-off point than an end in itself. So I'm consciously trying to avoid guidebook conventions here by being honest with you about the trail systems I'm familiar with, by not purporting to have firsthand knowledge of a trail I have never seen (it happens), and by suggesting approaches for experience that I'm curious about or—based on my experience, limitations, and time—would have enjoyed doing but couldn't.

For those riders who do want more guidance, I have inserted what I feel are the most requisite details. Increasing experience decreases the need for such detail as you grow accustomed to backcountry use, wilderness travel, repairs and first aid, sustenance, hydration, map orientation, and protection from the elements.

Finally, this book does not pretend to offer the "best of" all-terrain rides in the Adirondacks since that claim would imply that I have ridden all of the worthwhile trails there—something that in my estimation is probably impossible. The mountain routes that are currently open and legal in the Adirondack Wild Forest already represent near-infinite possibilities and are expected to change, as everything inevitably does, at a rate that will resist definition and comprehension by any one cyclist. You just can't have "the best of" something that's infinite. So to suggest that I'm offering you the best rides in the Adirondacks within these pages would be an unrealistic boast. Instead, these are the best of the trails I have personally ridden, which always turns out to be more than the 25 final tours. My strategy for approaching the huge and unwieldy Adirondack Park, with its millions of acres, was to ride where knowledgeable people, maps, and instinct led me and to write about each area that I liked.

Good, better, and best—there are tours that appropriate each definition in this book. But they're all in or above the category of "good." You'll enjoy the paved roads as much as the back roads and the trails as much as the dirt roads. And since there's not enough time to ride them all in one lifetime, don't just sit there: Get out and spin your wheels.

Notes for Using This Guide

Rating System

Each ride description is preceded by a rating that is intended to give you a rough idea of the difficulty of the trail. Be aware, however, that most trails contain both very ridable and quite challenging sections; I will point these out as necessary.

Beginner/intermediate

Suitable for riders with the most basic off-road background, such as pre-teens and inexperienced adults or seniors. Trails are mostly low mileage, flat, or slightly hilly with low aerobic demands, few obstacles, and a homogeneous treadway of cinder, pavement, or smooth dirt.

Intermediate/advanced

For experienced adult or teenaged riders who lack the confidence for or interest in managing highly challenging and technical terrain but have confidence and a willingness to improve on higher-mileage backcountry trails with varying treadway surfaces. Expect negotiable obstacles such as rocks, logs, streams, mud, steeper hills, washboard, loose sand, and descents. Riders should anticipate moderate aerobic output and have some knowledge of and/or experience with off-road technique.

Advanced/expert

The most challenging of routes requiring a high level of fitness; high aerobic output is a given. Trails include all of the preceding treadway types plus the possibility of slickrock, sidehills, drop-offs, and longer distances with few or no services between trailheads. A high familiarity with off-road technique and bike handling is required, and a corresponding awareness of emergency repairs, self-rescue, and survival skills may be called upon.

Riding Technique

Read up on climbing and descending if you haven't done so yet. Learn which brake lever operates which brake. Learn about out-of-saddle positions, pedal positions, brake feathering, and things like "letting go"—gaining enough speed to clear obstacles that would send you over the bars at lower speeds. (Books are available on the subject—see page 25.)

IMBA Rules of the Trail

These rules have been developed by the International Mountain Biking Association, and all riders would do well to follow them.
1. Ride on open trails only.
2. Leave no trace.
3. Control your bicycle.
4. Always yield trail.
5. Never spook animals.
6. Plan ahead.

Mileage

For reasons described below, the mileage markers in this book must be considered guidelines, not absolutes. They are given in tenths and in some cases hundredths of a mile. Don't expect your cyclometer to exactly reflect the book's mile measurements for any given tour. They won't. While the intent is to give an accurate, overall tour distance, individual readings for specified turns and landmarks will vary from your own. Accordingly, use the given mileage as a reference, and where it is suggested in the text, carry the appropriate maps and refer to them as well as to landmarks for direction finding.

Equipment

Cyclocomputers and Cyclometers
Cyclocomputers are among the more fidgety and accident-prone gadgets on the accessory list of bicycling. Most mountain bikes you'll see on the

trails today are not equipped with them. Off-road riders are not as concerned with mileage as touring bikers, and the excessive wiring, wheel, and spoke-mounted hardware is a liability in the brushy, bumpy, brash environment of the off-road cycle. In general, the more expensive and complicated these gadgets become, the less reliable they seem to be on mountain bikes. Wireless models may eliminate wire, but they have a larger fork-mounted sensor-transmitter than wired models. Having this much fragile mass low down on your fork is not always desirable. Also, proximity to whirring machinery (like your car's motor) may drive them wild. Wireless models are also known to interfere with heart-rate monitors and are susceptible to microwave transmission (cellular phones), although most manufacturers claim to have worked out these bugs. Thus, new "interference-free" models have appeared on the market.

Speed and distance readings are nice to have, but some of the other cycle computer features are gimmicky and redundant. Maximum and average speed, clock and stopwatch (what about your wristwatch?), dual interval timers, training summaries, programmable multiple bicycle calibration, calorie counters, and built-in heart-rate limit warnings are all useful training tools but quickly add to the complexity and distraction of the ride.

Even a reliable cyclometer is prone to inaccuracies. Differences in calibration when mounting (figuring the correct wheel circumference), surface wheel spin, car-rack wheel spin (remove your cycle computer while traveling), carrying your bike, and forgetting to reset (they are all prone to that particular human error) will all influence your readings. If you get a cyclometer, ask your dealer for the simplest, most reliable model (which is usually the cheapest), and let the dealer install it. Then, compare your trip distances with friends (and maps) to see if you're accurate. If you're not acceptably accurate with a map or measured mile, you'll need to recalibrate.

Tools and Flats

Going afield without tools is risky. You may be in for a long walk for want of just an adjustable or Allen head wrench. People walking their bikes in a state of dejection will often ask if you have a certain tool. An excellent, if not mandatory, investment, which you can shove into your wedge, bar, or frame pack and forget about, are the multitools offered by bicycle pro shops. Some are better than others—which you'll discover someday while trying to extract and replace a chain rivet with an inferior chain tool while sweat drips from your body and mosquitoes assault your back. Buy a good one. They contain almost everything you'll ever need "and nothing you don't" for minor trail repairs.

What they won't do, however, is fix flats. You've got to carry at least two tire levers and a patch kit if your tool set doesn't include them. You can carry an extra tube if you want, but still bring the patch kit. Spare tubes are cheap. Last, you're going to need a source to inflate your tire after a flat. If you know you've got a puncture, you can always add a little "slime" (patching goo) as you reinflate, which seals punctures up to about $^{3}/_{16}$ inch diameter. Then inflate with either your pump or CO_2 inflation device. The latter fit any valve, and some handle any size cartridge. Don't expect to achieve perfection on your first try with an inflator, however, and don't wait until you have a flat in the backcountry to learn! It takes a little practice. Until you're good at it, carry extra CO_2 cartridges. The only advantage inflators have over pumps is the speed of the fill. Otherwise, they lean toward the gimmicky.

Lighting systems
I don't use or recommend fixed lighting on a mountain bike unless your primary use is street riding. In that case, investing in a good system (and some can be quite expensive, costing over $200) may be worth it. For those rides in the backcountry that last until dark—and sometimes they do whether we planned it that way or not—it's best to carry a headlamp. These are very reliable and reasonably priced these days, and their main advantage is that they illuminate where you are looking—something you'll really come to appreciate if you ride uneven terrain at night. Another good thing to have is a taillight, like the kind that blink continuously and mount on a simple seat-post adaptor. With the combination of the headlamp and taillight, you'll be in good shape for backroad traffic. Be sure your taillight isn't obscured by your wedge pack, jacket, or rack baggage. Leave the reflectors that come with your new bike where they are. Look for other lightweight and reliable lights that you can carry easily.

Support Your Local Bike Shop
For reasons having to do with local trail advocacy and the advancement of the sport of mountain biking, I urge you to purchase your equipment

at your local bike shop. Bike shops are where trail advocacy begins. They're the little nerve centers through which all local ride and access information passes. Particularly in the Adirondacks, where the season is short, your local shop needs your support. If your shop doesn't have an item you want, they can get it for you.

Safety and Precautions

Many of these tours are in close proximity to vertical drops, steep trail-side ravines, and overhead rock. Precipitous and potentially hazardous terrain is home to the mountain bike, but your discretion must be exercised to ensure a happy and safe experience. Be especially alert when traveling with children. Be firm and repetitive with them, and insist on helmets. In fact, in New York State it's the law that children 14 and under *must* wear a helmet. Ride ahead of kids when potential hazards are discussed in the text. Walk when you're near danger.

Carry a small first-aid kit with several large Band-Aids, a gauze pad, and some antiseptic. Leave these at the bottom of your handlebar bag or underseat bag. You may not necessarily apply a Band-Aid to a small cut or abrasion, but kids really like them, and giving them the extra attention will help to maintain morale.

Carry extra food, water, and clothing. If you get lost, have a breakdown, or find yourself delayed for any reason, these items will help. Remember: Bicyclists are susceptible to exposure, too.

Biker's Checklist

Day Trips
full water bottles or backpack hydration system
cycling shorts
helmet
sunglasses
gloves
first-aid kit
matches and fire starter
whistle

lock
tire-repair tools and patch kit
pump or inflator
extra tube
basic tool kit
maps and compass
lunch/snack
sunscreen
insect repellent
raingear
headlamp
batteries

Optional but Useful Items (Especially for Longer Tours)
panniers
handlebar bag
rack strap
head- and taillight
journal
camera
towel/swimsuit
windbreaker

Maps

Adirondack Maps, Inc.
The first maps listed in each tour's subtitle information are those made by Adirondack Maps, Inc. (formerly Plinth, Quoin & Cornice, Associates), those colorful and user-friendly maps seen almost everywhere in Adirondack stores. These are the most readily available maps for your purposes. They were created by hikers for outdoors people and contain all the trail information you are likely to want or require. The beauty of this map set is that you can buy comprehensive map coverage for the Adirondack Park without great expense. If you tried to do the same thing using United States Geological Survey (USGS) maps, you'd not only be spending a fortune, but you'd have to carry several maps at a time for some individual tours. Also, the USGS has recently changed their series

maps names and sizes, so even finding the correct map for your tour can be time consuming—if you can find them at all (many quality outfitter shops stock local topographic maps). They are also in metric format now and don't cover the same (exact) areas that the previous series did. As a result, only a reference to USGS maps is given in the tour information, right after the Adirondack Map you'll need. Other maps are listed if helpful, including site handout maps, campground maps, and county road maps. Some trails are so self-guiding that you may be tempted to travel without a map, but I discourage such a practice because it will inevitably lead to some regret and, at best, inconvenience.

The maps in this book should provide the information you'll need, provided you stay on the trails included. However, it is always a good idea to carry a more detailed topographic map and a good compass with you, no matter what trail you're on.

The following is a list of the topographic maps currently published by Adirondack Maps:

> *The Adirondack Park*
> *Adirondack Canoe Map*
> *The Adirondacks: Central Mountains*
> *The Adirondacks: High Peaks Region*
> *The Adirondacks: Lake George Region*
> *The Adirondacks: Northwest Lakes*
> *The Adirondacks: West-Central Wilderness*

The price for each of the above maps is $4.95. Add an additional $1.50 for postage regardless of how many you order. New York State residents need to add 7 percent sales tax. Send a check or money order to: Adirondack Maps, Inc., PO Box 718, Market Street, Keene Valley, NY 12943; 518-576-9861; Web site: http://www.adirondackmaps.com; e-mail: AdackMaps@aol.com.

Adirondack Mountain Club Maps

The Adirondack Mountain Club (ADK) is also an excellent source of maps. Unlike the maps produced by Adirondack Maps, Inc., ADK's maps distinguish between public and private lands. This shouldn't be a problem, though, if you stay on the trails shown in this book and on the Adirondack Maps. Another advantage of ADK's maps is that they cover the entire forest preserve with just seven maps (they also cover the

Catskills, with one map, for a total of eight). ADK maps can be purchased with or without ADK's guidebook to the regions covered by the maps, for $5.95 each, with 20 percent off for club members.

ADK's Adirondack maps cover the High Peaks, Northern, Central, West-Central, Eastern, and Southern Adirondacks, as well as the Northville-Lake Placid Trail. There is a strong argument to be made in terms of the convenience of these maps, which fold up smaller and transport more easily than the larger Adirondack Maps, Inc., maps. All things considered, however, I have found that more shops consistently stock the big Adirondack Maps, Inc. maps than they do the ADK maps, perhaps because they appeal to a wider range of people outside the hiking and canoeing public.

United States Geological Survey (USGS) Maps

See my discussion of the pros and cons of these maps on pages 23 and 24.

Books

The following are all excellent introductions to the basic techniques of mountain biking:

The Complete Mountain Biker by Dennis Coello. New York: Lyons & Burford, 1989.

Sloane's Complete Book of All-Terrain Bicycles by Eugene A. Sloane. New York: Simon & Schuster, 1991.

Mountain Biking: The Complete Guide by the editors of *Sports Illustrated.*

Mountain Biking for Women by Robin Stuart and Cathy Jensen. Waverly, NY: Acorn Publishing, 1994.

A Woman's Guide to Cycling by Susan Weaver. Berkeley, Calif.: Ten Speed Press, 1991.

Cycling for Women by the editors of *Bicycling Magazine.* Emmaus, Pa.: Rodale Press, 1989.

The Adirondack Park Mountain Bike Preliminary Trail and Route Listing published by the Adirondack Mountain Club.

The Adirondack Park Mountain Bike Preliminary Trail and Route Listing— a large, blue, spiral-bound book, which you'll see almost everywhere books are sold in the Adirondacks—must be recognized as the first attempt to identify and define suitable mountain bike rides in the park.

Originally the product of a grant from the Adirondack North Country Association, the book's mission was to address the growing dilemma of exactly where ATBs could be legally used in the Adirondack Park. Interestingly, the dialogue between the Adirondack Park Agency, the DEC, and ANCA's Tourism Committee (which resulted in the publication) spawned the agreement between the park agency and the DEC to allow bikes on wild forest lands under a three-year trial study.

Because many of the trails in ADK's preliminary study were not actually ridden by bikers or reported on firsthand but were instead simply identified on maps and through the verbal recommendation of clubs, agencies, and individuals, it is difficult—and in many cases unreliable—for use as a trail guide (the study's authors state that "it is not intended to be all-encompassing or exhaustive in detail," and they provide that "conditions have not been surveyed on all trails . . . nor is the listing intended to replace a map, guidebook, or good judgment"). Conditions in the field will not necessarily be ridable, even though they are included in the study. Some of the trails may be nonexistent, underwater, barred by blowdowns, or otherwise designated "off-limits" when you get there. Many, I feel, are too environmentally sensitive for ATB use and should be removed from the book, even though they are technically legal (the Northwest Bay Trail, for example, both for its ecological sensitivity and user-group conflict potential). Discriminating cyclists will recognize such field conditions when they see them and will behave accordingly.

Nevertheless, I feel that the study is an excellent resource that anyone will benefit from referencing and enjoy using—provided you're aware of its limitations. There isn't a better inventory of Adirondack bike trails in existence and probably never will be. Future editions of this fascinating publication (now in the editorial hands of the Adirondack Mountain Club) promise to provide comprehensive information on forest and backcountry routes in the park.

I. WEST-CENTRAL WILDERNESS

1
The Train from Thendara

Location: *Herkimer County, Old Forge, Town of Webb lands*
Distance: *8.92 miles*
Terrain: *Gentle hills, some steep climbs, long flats*
Surface Conditions: *Dirt doubletrack and singletrack*
Rating: *Beginner/intermediate*
Maps: *Old Forge, Town of Webb Mountain Bike and Hiking Trail System, available from Tourist Information Center, Old Forge, NY 13420, 518-369-6983. Maps are also posted on the trail and available in Old Forge at many locations.*
Highlights: *This is the best-marked and -managed mountain-bike trail system in the Adirondacks, with access by car and the Adirondack Scenic Railroad.*

It's unheard of to find a publicly owned place such as this, where mountain bikers have been made so welcome that they're provided with a signed and marked trail system and a map that says, "We welcome you to a unique mountain bike experience where you will be able to enjoy the beauty of the Central Adirondack Region." To make this fascinating trail system even better, you get to access it via the Adirondack Scenic Railroad, a worthwhile outing in and of itself! This tour will appeal to your children and to family members who prefer easy riding on good quality "groomed" and graded trails.

While the loops described here do tend to be fairly long and involved for beginners, it's easy to design your own ride, modifying it to whatever distance and difficulty level you require. The best way to do that is to opt for a round-trip train ride and make up your own tour, which is a simple matter (at this time you have to pay full fare, anyway, even if you're riding only halfway). In the train loop described here, you get out at

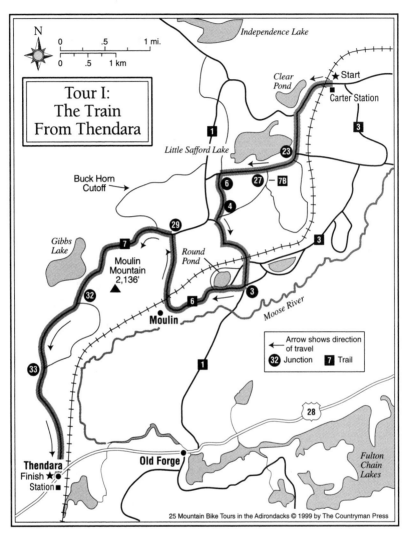

N

0   .5   1 mi.

0   .5   1 km

**Tour I:
The Train
From Thendara**

Independence Lake

*Clear
Pond*   ★ Start
■ Carter Station

1   **3**

Little Safford Lake   23

Buck Horn
Cutoff →

6   27 7B

4

29

*Gibbs
Lake*   7   *Round
Pond*   3

Moulin
Mountain
2,136'   ▲   6   3

32   *Moose River*

• Moulin

Arrow shows direction
of travel
32 Junction   7 Trail

33   1

28   *Fulton
Chain
Lakes*

Thendara
Finish ★   • Old Forge
Station ■

25 Mountain Bike Tours in the Adirondacks © 1999 by The Countryman Press

Carter Station, which is the train's present turnaround, and ride back to
Thendara (the elevation advantage isn't noticeable). You can also dis-
pense with the train ride completely to exit and enter the trail system
from Thendara on trail #6 in Old Forge via trail #1, as well as from Eagle
Bay via Rondaxe Road and trail #5.

Once inside the trail system from Carter Station, you can tour any number of easy, scenic loops and pick up the next train out. The train schedule is timed perfectly for that purpose and provides Old Forge Scenic Excursions at 10 AM, 11:30 AM, 1 PM, 2:30 PM, and 4 PM daily. Round trips to Carter Station take about an hour and a quarter. Special events excursions are offered on weekends and seasonally, with such themes as train robberies (they don't really kill the robbers at the end), fall foliage rides, a Hobo Weekend, the Halloween Express, and a Friday Night Special, which includes entertainment in the club car and a midnight return.

The Adirondack Scenic Railroad is a full-scale, diesel-powered passenger train, running under a permit from the New York State Department of Transportation. It's a project of the Adirondack Railway Preservation Society, a nonprofit corporation that offers annual memberships. This is the same train that ran briefly to Lake Placid during the 1980 Winter Olympics, and as of this writing it has introduced its Utica–Old Forge Round-Trip Service. For these longer runs, the refurbished coaches have both heat and air-conditioning, a full-service café car, and a gift shop. Flag stops are made at Holland Patent, Remsen, Forestport, Woodgate, and Otter Lake. Canoeists should take note that the train will also return them and their boat to an upstream put-in after they paddle the Moose River. Expansion northward is planned so that one day you'll be able to ride the train to Beaver River on Stillwater Reservoir and beyond. No matter how you do it, ride this train. It goes slowly, 6–7 mph (but 40 mph on the Thendara–Utica run), so you can sightsee appropriately and search the swamps for moose. It's a perfect rainy-day activity, too, if you're camping in the area and looking for some diversion.

To reach Thendara Station, which is about 1.5 miles south of Old Forge on NY 28, take the New York State Thruway to Exit 31 at Utica and follow NY 12N to NY 28 (north). From the Adirondack Northway (I-87), take Exit 23 at Warrensburg to NY 28 (west) and Old Forge. Park in the Thendara Station parking lot, and get ready. (There's a gift shop, rest rooms, and a food vendor here.) When you're packed, the conductors will hoist your bikes into the freight car.

Relax for the ride north, past the Moose River and through the trail system you'll be returning on. You'll most likely see other cyclists or hikers on these popular trails. An interpretive dialogue runs on the coach's sound system, telling you all about the Adirondack Park and the train's history.

Off loading at Carter Station

Arrive at Carter station, and disembark.

0.0 **Cross the tracks in front of the station, and follow the dirt road (trail #7).**

Disregard the NO TRESPASSING signs—this is a legal thoroughfare. The road is flat and easy.

0.28 **Turn left at a Y, where you'll see a sign kiosk. Head toward Little Safford Lake.**

0.6 **Cross Little Safford Lake outlet over a small bridge.**

The railroad berm is up to your left. When blooming, fireweed frames a good view of the lake.

0.7 **Arrive at junction #23 of the trail system.**

Note that not all junctions are marked; prepare to be somewhat confused by the apparently conflicting information given by the trail signs, and follow these directions. It will all make sense in the end. At this junction you'll see the tracks and a crossing on your left.

Turn to the right here, following the shore of Little Safford Lake.

Shortly, excellent views of the lake open up on your right.

1.23 **Come up a gentle incline to junction #27, where you'll see signs to Big Moose as well as to Old Forge (pointing in both directions). Keep going straight, leaving trail #7b to your left.**

2.12 **Cross the pipeline intersection, #6p, continuing straight. You'll be joining the uphill section of the pipeline momentarily.**

2.20 **Arrive at junction #6. Turn left. Climb to the top of a hill.**

2.43 **At an H intersection, turn left, crossing the bar of the H, and turn right in front of a yellow pipeline valve post.**

You're on the pipeline. The surface is excellent.

3.01 **Pass an unmarked trail on the right.**

3.05 **Arrive at junction #4, which shows Old Forge to your left, Thendara to your right (no mileages are given), and, among other destinations, trail #7 to your left. Go left, even though it doesn't say Thendara is to the left. You're on trail #1.**

3.2   Cross the tracks, and continue straight ahead.

You'll see lots of bike tracks. Wave at the train, which may likely be going by or which you may continually be hearing in the distance.

3.29 At junction #3, go right.

This is a four-way intersection, where trail #1 goes straight ahead to Old Forge, and is the quickest way out at this point (aside from flagging down the train) if you've had enough for any reason. Trail #3 to Eagle Bay and Big Moose goes to the left.

Follow right, on trail #6 to Thendara.

3.41 At an unmarked T, go left.

3.52 Reaching a three-way intersection, which marks the beginning of the Round Pond Loop, go straight, continuing on trail #6.

You get a view of Round Pond on your right through the forest.

3.76 Bear left at a Y, next to a sign for Thendara, Round Pond Loop.

The sign is confusing. It looks like you should go straight, but don't do it.

3.83 Cross a tiny wetland, over a culvert.

4.34 Cross the railroad tracks at Moulin, the site of an old Canadian mill that no longer exists.

4.7   At junction #29, the most confusing trail junction in the Adirondacks, turn left, climb for a moment. Stay on trail #7.

4.75 Pass straight through the trail intersection to Buck Horn Cut Off, and continue climbing up the shoulder of Moulin Mountain.

It's not strenuous.

5.45 Pass an unmarked road on the right, then a mire, then an old, abandoned Willy's jeep on your right.

5.55 Start heading downhill.

6.22 At junction #32, go straight ahead toward Thendara on trail #7.

The left also goes to Thendara, and it looks like a better trail, but you'd go down a steep hill that way and have to regain significant elevation afterward. Stay on trail #7. I prefer this section of trail to the dirt roads, even though it's a slower surface. It's more like a path through the forest now, overgrown with grass, getting little use from vehicles because of the wilderness area barrier ahead and the poor condition of the bridge ahead.

6.22 *Go straight here at junction #32.*

The map shows a scenic lookout just ahead on the left, but the trail wasn't marked, and the one I suspected was the trail looked so overgrown, I decided to pass. If the trail's cleaned up, I'm told the lookout is well worth a stop.

7.5 *Now at junction #33, you're in a clearing with some views, Go right, crossing the bridge.*

8.2 *At a Y, go left.*

The trail to the right enters the Ha-De-Ron-Dah Wilderness Area and as such is off-limits. See the trail signs and map kiosk on your right for details.

There are no signs suggesting what might be to your left, but turn left, anyway.

8.27 *Go past a barrier gate.*

A sign for trail #6 is on the right as you come out. The tracks are on your left.

Follow this dirt road until reaching NY 28.

8.7 *Arrive at NY 28. Thendara Station is across the highway and to the right.*

Traffic is not user-friendly here. Use extreme caution, bear right along the shoulder, and cross when it's safe. (Going left instead at mile 8.7 and under the railroad bridge isn't any better.)

8.92 *You're back at the train station parking lot.*

The Remsen–Lake Placid Travel Corridor and its right-of-way was constructed by William Seward Webb in 1892. It was operated by the New York Central Railroad until 1965, when regular passenger service ceased. Penn Central, created by the merger of the New York Central and Pennsylvania Railroads, stopped its freight service in 1965. Now the state owns the corridor, and management plans will provide for the future recreational and passenger service.

Camping Permits and General Information

Forest Ranger Headquarters: NYSDEC, 225 N. Main St., Herkimer, NY 13350: 315-866-6330

Thendara Station, Old Forge, NY: 315-369-6290

Union Station, Utica, NY: 315-724-0700

Special Events: Web site: www.Adirondacktravel.com/scenicRR.HTML; e-mail: train@telenet.net

Inlet Information Center, Inlet, NY: 315-357-5501; www.inletny.com/

Old Forge Information/Central Adirondack Association: 315-369-6983; Web site: www.adirondacktravel.com

Bike Shops

Pedals and Petals, NY 28, 176N, Inlet, NY: 315-357-3281; e-mail: pedpet@telenet.net; Web site: www.tvenet.com/pedalsandpetals/

Pine's Country Store, NY 28, Box 339, Indian Lake, NY: 518-648-5212

2
Moss, Bubb, and Sis Lakes

Location: *Herkimer County, Town of Webb, Fulton Chain Wild Forest*
Terrain: *Gently rolling*
Distance: *2.6-mile loop connected to a 4.2-mile return spur; total tour,
7 dirt miles, plus 4 road miles to complete loop.*
Surface Conditions: *Pine needle–covered dirt doubletrack, singletrack*
Rating: *Beginner (Moss Lake); intermediate/advanced (spur to NY 28)*
Maps: *The Adirondacks: West-Central Wilderness; USGS: Eagle Bay; ADK:
West Central Region*
Highlights: *Moss Lake is a very gentle, scenic beginner's tour, with sev-
eral camping sites, swimming, and primitive facilities. Bubb Lake is a
wildernesslike lake on a strong beginner to intermediate trail. The tour
is very close to Eagle Bay and connects by trail to the Old Forge/
Town of Webb Mountain Bike and Hiking Trail System.*

These two friendly and attractive lake trails have seen some well-
deserved publicity from the recreational media and have grown in popularity since the state reinherited this location from the warrior class of the
Mohawk Indians. You can tell your kids that there may still be a few of
them around, just to keep them pedaling. The appeal of this lake system
is multifaceted, but a good deal of it derives from their convenient locations, just a few miles above the fabled Fourth Lake of the Fulton Chain
of lakes, and their proximity to Eagle Bay, Old Forge, and Inlet, with all
the excitement that these alluring lake towns have to offer at the height
of tourist season. Moss Lake is regularly frequented by young campers
and mature flower sniffers. Couples walk arm-in-arm, dizzily inhaling
the fragrant pine woods. Children especially love the pine-shaded trails
of the Adirondacks, the endlessness and mystery of big lakes, the boat

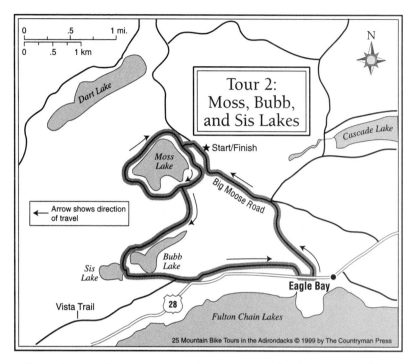

rides and marauding raccoons at the campgrounds, the promise of face-planting a cone at the Tastee-Freeze, and, finally, getting some real "Indian stuff" at the tourist shops. "And tomorrow," you can announce at your campfire, "we're going to ride our bikes around a lake. Or two!"

Almost anyone can ride around Moss Lake in a relaxed half hour, slowing for every bird call or pink lady's slipper, stopping to dangle their legs from the warm planks of the southwest outlet, and bending over backward to see the tops of craggy, old-growth white pines. After that loop, you can corkscrew your way over a smooth, slinky singletrack to a dark wild-forest lake—where, according to local wisdom, "nobody goes"—finishing with a scary but short downhill that ends on the flat sand route back up to Eagle Bay (or you can ride back to Moss Lake for a tamer version). Children (I'd venture to say 7 or above with some biking experience) will do fine going around Moss Lake, which was once a bridle path to the erstwhile estate, but only youngsters with a brave heart, a good bike with tuned-up brakes, and a real helmet should be encouraged to tackle the mostly forgiving Bubb route, unless you turn around at the bridge (read on). Here is mountain biking in its essence— fragrant woods, the thrill of singletrack, wilderness scenery, and a sense of personal achievement and elation. No sweat or agony. Even adventuresome touring cyclists mounted on hybrids will enjoy the tour (although mountain bikes will be more comfortable), and it has been confided to me by one particular hammerhead in town that this is her "preferred" workout ride. So, go ahead. Take a look. Maybe it'll be yours, as well. (If you're alone, park at Moss Lake access and ride the whole thing, returning on Big Moose Road from NY 28 for a tour of about 10 miles.)

From NY 28, above Old Forge and south of Inlet, you'll find the trailhead access easily; go 2.3 miles north of Eagle Bay on Big Moose Road; and the trailhead will be on the left. A big parking area, an orientation signboard, and a history of the area greet you at the trailhead. Right at that point, hop on your bikes. Note that the bridle path goes both left and right. I suggest starting out by going left, which breaks up the minimal elevation gain into small pieces instead of lump sums. It's a good idea to register right here at the trailhead.

Moss Lake

0.0 *Turn left at the signboard, onto the path.*

This is a wide, easy doubletrack. Watch for hikers and strollers. There may even be a horse or two around. If you see them, stop your bikes until they pass. It shows good manners and is accepted IMBA trail etiquette (see IMBA's rules of the road in the Introduction). You'll notice a few trails going off to the right, toward the lake, which you're allowed to explore. Follow yellow trail markers.

0.15 *Walk through a short sand pit and hop back on your bike.*

0.5 *Cross a bridge over a small feeder creek.*

0.7 *Arrive at a Y. Take the right fork, which goes straight ahead.*

You'll see signs on a tree to your right, indicating directions and distances. To the left are: Bubb Lake (0.7 mile), Sis Lake (1.4 miles), the Vista Trail (2.1 miles), and NY 28 (2.8 miles). Straight ahead is the parking area you came from at 1.8 miles. Also, the entire loop distance around Moss Lake is given at 2.5 miles.

Continue.

1.2 *Arrive at a bridge over the outlet in the southwesternmost area of the lake.*

At this time there are two very large white pines on the northwest side of the bridge and a grove of pines on a knoll to your left, also across the bridge. (The water here is about 3 feet deep.) This is the only spot that's close to the lake on the bridle path, but to get to others, follow the little trails you'll see heading off to the right. A few small hills are coming and some small rocks in the trail. Continue along until arriving back at the starting point.

2.6 *You're back at the trailhead starting point.*

This completes the Moss Lake Loop. Most riders who are familiar with the area will have either taken the Bubb Lake Trail out and back or ridden straight through. If you're an advanced rider looking for more distance, don't miss this trail.

Bubb Lake/Sis Lake

0.0 *Begin at the parking area (as for Moss Lake), turn left.*

0.7 *Arrive at the trail intersection. Follow to the left, in the direction of Bubb and Sis Lakes.*

This is a smooth, fast singletrack ride with few if any obstructions, blowdowns, large rocks, or holes. It winds along until reaching a creek.

1.1 *Cross the creek, where you'll see a fish barrier dam. This tiny capillary is a headwater of the North Branch, Moose River.*

1.3 *Come to the edge of Bubb Lake, where a hemlock grove meets the shore within a primitive campsite.*

This is a fairly large lake, with no structures. Trout were rising as I stopped to take a look around.

Continue through the woods.

The trail begins to change in character to short little descents and rises, offering a few roots and rocks as minor technical challenges.

2.1 *Cross a bridge between Bubb and Sis Lakes, where at this* *writing there's a tremendous cherry tree on the right, just before you cross.*

You'll almost touch the tree with your right shoulder, since it's invading the bridge's space somewhat. A long lightning crack runs down the north side of its trunk, which you can see from the bridge. Maybe it won't land on the bridge when it goes, but it looks as if it might. Cross the bridge and take a look at the primitive campsite on the left. This area is legal for camping, since it has been "established" (impacted). But there is considerable soil and vegetation damage here, and this site, along with other shore-side sites, may be closed in the future as a result. So to be on the safe side, check to make sure it is still legal by searching for the DEC CAMP HERE discs.

Strong beginners will have had no problems up to this point, but the rest of the trail is rockier, not nearly as pretty, and ends with a short but challenging descent. This is the best place to turn around and go back to Moss Lake if that is your intention. If you are feeling up to it, you're only 0.9 mile from NY 28.

Proceed. A few sections of trail are wet and rocky now.

2.6 *At a Y, a lesser trail turns left and goes down to the edge of Bubb Lake. You go right, following yellow markers, on a somewhat rocky, corduroyed section of trail.*

2.8 *Pass the Vista Trail on your right as the trail you're on gets rockier and more challenging.*

Advanced riders will savor this little rocky run, but less confident riders should walk. This is the only "hard" part of the trail and is the major reason why people don't ingress from this trailhead. It just looks horrendous. Beginners can expect a challenge here, and should be advised to walk the difficult stretches. Smaller children will become demoralized as the descent to NY 28 begins. If you're at all in doubt, turn around now.

2.9 *Pull out onto the sandy bike path next to NY 28.*

There are signs just as you exit the woods, but the only indication of the trail's existence from the road is a small yellow arrow on the usual brown post. This egress is 1.5 miles south of the intersection of Big Moose Road and NY 28 in Eagle Bay.

If you're riding back to the Moss Lake trailhead over the road, follow the sand trail to your left until reaching Eagle Bay. Then go left again on Big Moose Road.

4.6 *Arrive in Eagle Bay; turn left on Big Moose Road.*

6.9 *Arrive at the trailhead (total with Moss Lake Loop, about 10 miles).*

Camping Permits and General Information:

Forest Ranger Headquarters: NYSDEC, 225 North Main Street, Herkimer, NY 13350: 315-866-6330

Old Forge Information/Central Adirondack Association: 315-369-6983; Web site: www.adirondacktravel.com

Bike Shops

Pedals and Petals, NY 28, 176N/PO Box 390, Inlet, NY: 315-357-3281; e-mail: pedpet@telenet.net; Web site: www.tvenet.com/pedalsand-petals/

Pine's Country Store, NY 28, Box 339, Indian Lake, NY: 518-648-5212

3

Wakely Gate to Carry Lean-to

Location: *Town of Arietta, Moose River Plains Wild Forest*
Distance: *9.8 miles round-trip*
Terrain: *Gently rolling*
Surface conditions: *Sand and dirt roads*
Rating: *Intermediate/advanced*
Maps: *The Adirondacks: West-Central Wilderness; USGS: Indian Lake*
Highlights: *Carry Lean-to; remote setting; boat and canoe area; free camping*

This is one of the several great rides you'll discover in the Moose River Recreation Area (see the Black Fly Challenge, Tour #6, for directions and specific information on the MRRA). There are so many intriguing, off-beat, and remote tours within this particular wild forest that you'll have a hard time figuring out where you want to explore next. But you won't have a hard time coming back. This spot may just become your newest favorite place in the Adirondacks.

Riders of the Moose will need to exercise vigilance in terms of sticking to the legal Moose River Wild Forest. This area is bounded by the West Canada Lakes Wilderness Area. Make sure that any forays you plan beyond the trails in the tour do not trespass onto wilderness lands. You may want to pick up the DEC area pamphlet for more information. Forest rangers are serious about these regulations, and violations will likely result in a summons. The day I visited Wakely, rangers arrested an out-of-state gentleman for chopping down dead standing trees (only "dead-and-down" trees can be cut for firewood on state lands). These and similar regulations are designed to preserve the natural, forever-wild setting of the woods.

The tour through Wakely Gate and into Carry Lean-to can be staged

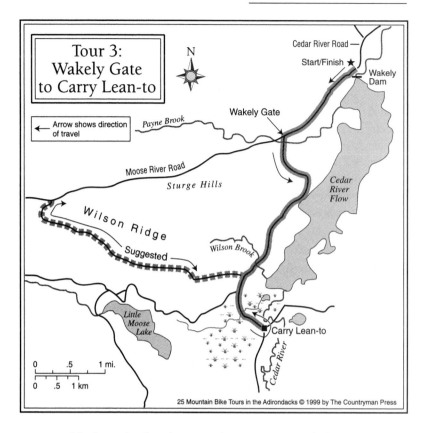

Tour 3:
Wakely Gate
to Carry Lean-to

N

Cedar River Road —
Start/Finish ★
Wakely
Dam

Arrow shows direction
of travel

Payne Brook

Wakely Gate

Moose River Road

Sturge Hills

*Cedar
River
Flow*

Wilson Ridge

Suggested

Wilson Brook

*Little
Moose
Lake*

Carry Lean-to

Cedar River

0   .5   1 mi.

0   .5   1 km

25 Mountain Bike Tours in the Adirondacks © 1999 by The Countryman Press

most readily from the free (primitive) campsite at Wakely Dam Ranger Headquarters. You can leave your car there and ride out through the gate, heading southwest, toward the Limekiln Gate. Stop at the register and enter your vehicle ID and plate number, plus your destination. You might ask the resident ranger about other places to ride, about the fish, wildlife, bugs (the place is loaded with all of these), or other concerns you might have. The ranger can also give you up-to-date trail information. Blowdowns, excessive standing water, mud, and reports of "Old Slewfoot" haunting the Carry Lean-to for leftovers may convince you to ride elsewhere that day. I did see the bear. As I was riding back to Wakely Dam from this very tour, a very large bear was standing in the middle of the road. It just looked at me, unconcerned. I was not, however. As I fumbled for my camera, the bear—200 feet distant—took a decisive step toward me and leveled a stare at me. My fight-or-flight thing kicked in heavily, and I started to turn my Y-bike around for a serious sprint. Bears may be able to outrun you on foot, but a scared mountain biker on a dirt road? I don't think so. (Just don't look back.) The bear bolted, all right, before I could turn around. His direction was dead east, into the woods, downhill. When I reported the incident to the ranger, he said, "Oh, boy. He'll be in camp tonight!" Black bears are generally no cause for concern in such situations. They're afraid of you, and you're lucky if you get to see one. It's important to follow the recommended procedures for handling food in campsites, though, if you don't want a face-to-face encounter with an animal whose foul breath will only be the beginning of a very bad night.

0.0 *Leave Wakely Dam (you can drive to Wakely Gate, saving the 1.2-mile road approach, but parking and security is minimal). Pedal up Moose River Road.*

1.2 *Turn left at the gate.*

There are trail signs here, a stop barrier, and blue trail markers. Follow the old logging road.

1.4 *Cross over Payne Brook on this fast doubletrack, and follow on some downhill that can be wet and slippery.*

2.4 *As the light above Cedar River Flow begins to radiate through the trees, you'll arrive at a primitive campsite with a fire ring, on your left.*

A series of very small meadows follows—probably old log decking areas—speckled with wildflowers. The forest type varies from open hardwoods to tight conifer stands. The hardwoods tunnel the trail for some distance. The treadway turns from wide doubletrack to twin spaghetti singletracks. Ferns and berry bushes are invading the track here and there, which will help to brush the mosquitoes off your legs.

3.65 *Cross Wilson Brook.*

Multicolored, knee-high hawkweeds whiz by like Hollywood renditions of light speed. Clumsy horseflies bash into your helmet and are seen no more. Dense and fragrant balsam firs caress your mosquito bites.

4.00 *At a Y, bear left.*

Carry Lean-to, overlooking the Cedar River

The trail to your right would take you over Wilson Ridge and out to Moose River Road again, but it's steep. If you want a bigger ride, you can add that mileage on, legally (it's still wild forest), but think about starting there, coming downhill, and riding out on the trail you're on. It would be far easier than going out that way.

4.25 *In a mature spruce-fir forest, a* WILDERNESS AREA *sign appears on your right. Keep on truckin'.*

4.45 *Cross a plank bridge over a nameless and serene wetland outlet.*

There are limited views of Buck and Little Moose Mountains here. At this time, the old bridge lies under water just upstream, lodged against the banks. Snowmobiles are starting to rip up the new bridge somewhat.

4.8 *Pass a vague, grassy path on your left.*

This is the trail to Carry Pond, but you can't ride there without fording the Cedar River. If you want to ford, it isn't that deep, and the trail to Carry Pond is very good, though short. On your right in a few more feet, trail signs appear at a Y. Mileages are given for Cedar River Headquarters, Stephens Pond Lean-to, and Blue Mountain Lake. To the right, a NO BIKES sign heads the trail into the West Canada Lakes Wilderness Area. On your left, eye-high to a short biker, is a LEAN-TO sign. Go for it, downhill.

4.9 *Arrive at the lean-to, which is situated on a bend in the Cedar River.*

Here I found instant oatmeal, soup packages, and a can of kidney beans (chili again?). There was also a thoughtful stash of paper goods—plates, cups, napkins, toilet paper, etc. Planning a hermitage? You might want to look here. I perused the camp's journal—an old salt-and-pepper composition book with a DEC decal on the front that is maintained by lean-to adopters—until the bugs drove me away. It seems a favorite pastime for hunters bivouacking here is to plink at ducks in the river.

Carry Lean-to is a lonely, deeply silent spot, awkwardly situated in an area unattractive in and of itself, densely foliated, with a singular winsome, upriver view. The lean-to is an off-hand construction, perhaps resulting from an excess of cut logs; the privy door now hangs by one hinge, and it's crowded with advancing brush. A trail to the east dead-ends in a hummocky spruce stand, sprinkled with 9mm shell casings, where old bear bags and assorted litter hang from small trees. A promising footpath past the privy, lined in-season with white-blooming bunchberry and flowering oxalis, wanders into dissolution among the backwoods, where standing trees have been cut for firewood. A few old steel hoops, a hank of wire rope, fern-cloaked boulders, an overstory of black cherry—it's a mixed montage of nature's best and man's worst.

A path in front of the lean-to leads to the slow-running river, where alders with white flowers crowd the sandy bank and brilliant daisies and spice-scented tansy entice curious, friendly butterflies; where, seated on the shards of someone's forgotten tarpaulin, I could hear muffled sounds of running water and the cry of some unknown bird.

Return the way you came.

Camping Permits and General Information

Forest Ranger Headquarters: NYSDEC, 701 South Main Street, Box 458, Northville, NY 12134: 518-863-4545

Old Forge Information/Central Adirondack Association: 315-369-6983/ Web site: www.adirondacktravel.com

Bike Shops

Pedals and Petals, NY 28, 176N/PO Box 390, Inlet, NY: 315-357-3281; e-mail: pedpet@telenet.net; Web site: www.tvenet.com/pedalsandpetals/

Pine's Country Store, NY 28, Box 339, Indian Lake, NY: 518-648-5212

4
Woodhull Lake Loop

Location: *Oneida and Herkimer Counties, Towns of Webb, Ohio, and Forestport, Black River Wild Forest*
Distance: *24 miles*
Terrain: *Remote, hilly*
Surface Conditions: *Dirt roads in poor condition, singletrack, and pavement*
Rating: *Intermediate/advanced*
Maps: *The Adirondacks: West-Central Wilderness; USGS: Woodgate and McKeever; ADK: Trails of the Adirondack West-Central Region*
Highlights: *Unlimited exploring opportunities; lean-to camping*

The Black River Wild Forest Area represents one of the largest untapped regions for ATB riders in the Adirondack Park. It's highlighted in maps that hang on bike shop walls, it's present in several publications and handouts, and it's located conveniently right off NY 28 at Woodgate. If your intention is to find an area where you can ride all weekend without retracing your tracks much, this is the place to come. Dirt roads, legal foot trails, and snowmobile routes comprise most of the forest thoroughfares. There are few if any secondary roads. This tour combines backwoods and road miles for a fairly strenuous intermediate to advanced tour.

Find Bear Creek Road in Woodgate, which is on NY 28 about 18 miles south of Old Forge. For specific directions to the region, consult "Train from Thendara" (Tour #1). Set your car's odometer to zero. At the four-way intersection in Woodgate, turn right (east) onto Bear Creek Road. Immediately on your right, pass a pair of hand-wrought log cabins. The paved road continues through stands of Scotch pine (the ones with the tan lower bark), and eventually deteriorates in surface quality.

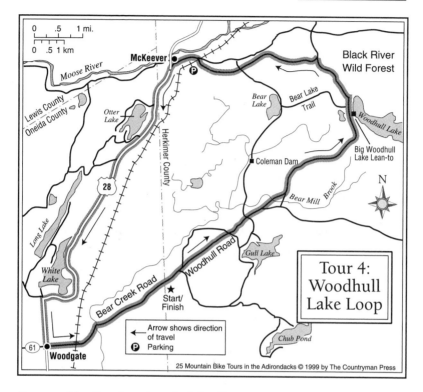

Pass an old railroad station. At 1.1 miles pass Sears Road on your right, and then pass Turk Road. At 3.1 miles you'll arrive at the Black River Wild Forest/Bear Creek Trailhead Parking Area. Here, an intricate trail map displays the interior's matrix of jeep roads, hiking and skiing trails, and snowmobile trails. The trails—except, of course, the ones you want—are very well marked. Be sure to carry a map or you may become lost in this large wild forest beyond your "wildest" dreams. Take the usual precautions regarding equipment and preparations (see the introduction). If you have a shuttle, park it at the McKeever Trailhead in, of all places, McKeever, which will save you the road mileage along NY 28. After a long slog in the backcountry, I like the feeling of riding a few road miles, especially on this section of road, which has wide shoulder and good scenery. It also tends to have pretty fast traffic, so watch yourself.

0.0 *From the parking area, follow the jeep road, a continuation at Bear Creek Road, which will become Woodhull Road beyond.*

49

> *Follow signs to Big Woodhull Lake Lean-to, at 7.6 miles, whether you intend to visit the lean-to or not.*

This is your direction of travel. A possible shortcut (unresearched) to Big Woodhull Lake exists ahead in the Coleman Dam–Bear Lake Trail, but a significant wetland along the east edge of Bear Creek merits discretion, particularly in wet periods. Many bikers meet with ill favor from the mud damsel (myself not excepted) when they forget that snowmobile trails are intended for use when most of that stuff is solid (lakes included). Read your maps carefully to determine if a long, mucky portage that hikes like dog chow is really what you're looking for. Potholes and mud greet you on the jeep road. You can imagine what the swamps are like.

0.3 *At a Y, take the left fork, following signs for Woodhull Lake.*

Gull Lake and Chub Pond is to your right, and the trail looks good, but I don't believe the mileages on the signs. It appears accurate that North Lake Road is at 11.5 miles on that trail, however. Tempted?

2.04 *A rocky, washed-out trail heads off to your right. Stay on the trail you're on.*

2.3 *Pass a primitive campsite on your right.*

The potholes in this road are insidious and menacing. The loamy soil is not absorbent, so rainwater persists for days. This is a no-frills, logged-over forest of ravaged stature, having been cut hard and relegated to the second-growth back burner in terms of forest management. In the parlance of the gypsy logger, this was a "take the best and leave the rest" job.

The jeep road meanders, climbing, and in spite of the mudholes whose soft edges threaten to side slump you into their depths, you can cruise on your middle ring most of the time. If you don't mind the splash, make that "all the time." There's nothing like soggy Lycra to keep you moving. Here's where you'll appreciate a pair of self-draining mountain biking shoes (they do exist!).

2.73 *Pass a trail to your left, which you can miss (but it won't matter) if you're not paying attention.*

This is the trail to Bear Lake, and it looks seductively ridable from this vantage point. I can't say, not having ridden it. A sign a few feet into the woods reads CAUTION LOG TRUCKS, then next to that, NO MOTOR VEHICLES (welcome to the forest preserve). Between 3 and 4 miles, the trail climbs a low grade.

3.5 **You arrive at an important Y. Go left, toward the Bear Lake Trail, Big Woodhull Lake Lean-to (5.9 miles), and your ultimate destination, the McKeever Parking Area (11 miles).**

To your right, a trail goes into the woods for about 10 feet, and then forks. The right fork is unmarked, while the left shows the destinations Sand Lake Falls and North Lake. On a tree in front of you there's an alligator crossing sign! To the left, your route takes you past a municipal school crossing sign, and then another that says VILLAGE OF MILLBROOK, POP. ZERO, DRY TOWN, which probably suggests something about the seasonal residents of a hunting shanty you'll see ahead.

Stay left, leaving the building to your right. Drift downhill.

3.69 **Cross Bear Mill Brook, a diamond-clear, moss-laden run of little pools.**

4.20 **At a T, keep going straight.**

A blowndown trail on your left heads into Coleman Dam, Bloodsucker Pond, and Bear Lake. If you're in a risk-taking mood, this is an alternate route, but now no longer a shortcut, to Big Woodhull Lake. The trail ahead is good. The treadway is much improved, probably owing to the fact that Bear Mill Brook bridge is currently too light for big trucks. Nevertheless, you see the CAUTION LOG TRUCKS sign again. The trail assumes a narrower, more pathlike character now. Some ugly rusted snowmobile signs appear as oil can bottoms nailed to the trees. The forest quality improves markedly.

6.0 **At a T, a smaller trail than the one you're on enters an abominable-looking wetland. There's presently no hint as to the trail's destination. Go left onto it.**

You can avoid a drubbing if you go 50 feet past the trail to a herd path that skirts the muck. Going straight here instead of going left, even though it looks like a better trail, can lead to all sorts of trouble: There's no egress, the road soon enters the private lands of the Adirondack League Club, and 2.5 miles later crosses a dam on Remsen Point Bay of Woodhull Lake (elevation 1,879'). Then you're really lost.

6.13 *With the wetland to your left, cross a plank bridge over a doubletrack trail that is fairly well established and identified with snowmobile trail markers.*

6.2 *Leave a swampy area to your right, where a small pond exists in periods of high water.*

Slog through a wetland up to your knees in places, or bushwhack around its edges. If you're wet already, it won't matter.

7.09 *Pass a trail sign pointing out the Big Woodhull Lake Lean-to, and cross a small bridge.*

You'll see trail signs for Remsen Falls, Woodhull Mt. Summit, and McKeever Parking Area (5.4 miles straight ahead). The lean-to is 0.3 mile from this spot. Just beyond the trail signs, in your direction of travel, the Bear Lake Trail goes to the left, following yellow markers.

Continue straight.

7.4 *Go through a stop barrier.*

Pass a good-looking unmarked trail that goes to the right, probably to Wolf Lake Landing. You begin to descend, and a few long, memorable sections of rock-hopping follow.

8.88 *At a T, continue left.*

Trail signs indicate Remsen Falls to the right. Now this sandy, hard flat trail ascends easily. The trail's contour varies from here, and you cross a few plank bridges and pass a few unnamed trails and primitive campsites.

12.2 *Arrive at the Big Woodhull Trailhead Parking Area (McKeever Parking Area), and go straight.*

To the right as you enter the parking lot, an attractive dirt road leads to a barrier gate and trail signs for the Bear Lake Trail, Remsen Falls, Big Woodhull Lake, Woodhull Mountain, and the Sand Lake Falls Trail.

12.61 *Cross the railroad tracks, passing the old station house on your left.*

13.05 *Arrive at NY 28 and go left (west) onto the wide shoulder, riding in the westbound lane (that is, in the same direction the traffic is moving).*

20.9 *Turn left onto Bear Creek Road in Woodgate.*

24.0 *Arrive at your car.*

Camping Permits and General Information

Forest Ranger Headquarters: NYSDEC, 225 North Main Street, Herkimer, NY 13350: 315-866-6330

Old Forge Information/Central Adirondack Association: 315-369-6983; Web site: www.adirondacktravel.com

Bike Shops

Pedals and Petals, NY 28, 176N, Inlet, NY: 315-357-3281; e-mail: ped-pet@telenet.net.; Web site: www.tvenet.com/pedalsandpetals/

Pine's Country Store, NY 28, Box 339, Indian Lake, NY: 518-648-5212

5

The SuperDuper Trail Ride

Location: *Herkimer County, Eagle Bay, Fulton Chain Wild Forest*
Distance: *12 miles round-trip*
Terrain: *Long flats along an abandoned railroad corridor*
Surface Conditions: *Dirt doubletrack*
Rating: *Beginner*
Maps: *USGS: Eagle Bay; Old/Forge, Town of Webb Mountain Bike and Hiking Trail System, available from Tourist Information Center, Old Forge, NY 13420 (518-369-6983). Maps are posted on the trail also, and available in the Old Forge and Inlet area at many locations.*
Highlights: *Easy, flat, scenic, entry-level family or exercise tour with places to relax and have a picnic as well as gain access to the interior Old Forge Mountain Bike Trail System*

Tour #5 (which I call the SuperDuper Trail) is another of the remarkable trails that characterize the Old Forge/Town of Webb Mountain Bike and Hiking Trail System, and helps to bolster the incontestable claims that this area is indeed the "Mountain Biking Capital of the Adirondacks"!

This is one of the best beginner trails I've ever seen. It is a safe, flat, scenic tour that for most of its length follows alongside NY 28, weaving in and out of the woods, occasionally yielding views of Fourth Lake, and passing a large pond and wetland where you can have lunch or just sit and ponder while your kids throw rocks into the water. No part of this trail is too isolated for those unaccustomed to remote woods, and the treadway is so fair and forgiving that you will be able to do the distance without having to get off your bike even once. Parents with small children will love this ride (and the kids will, too), while solo riders who may feel uncomfortable in a more remote setting will feel very secure.

The SuperDuper is a little supermarket at the corner of NY 28 and Big

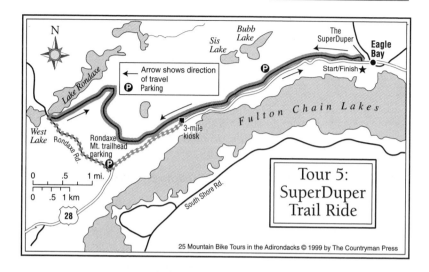

Tour 5:
SuperDuper
Trail Ride

25 Mountain Bike Tours in the Adirondacks © 1999 by The Countryman Press

Moose Road, in Eagle Bay. It is here that this super-duper trail ride begins, but don't expect to find trail signs or even the trail without looking around a bit. If you're really struggling to find it, follow along next to NY 28 going west, toward Old Forge, looking to your right, and you'll see the trail within a tenth of a mile. It's surprising, and sort of an inconvenience, that this trail is neither signed nor identified here, but once you're on it, you can't get lost. You will eventually run across a map kiosk with trail information at the 3-mile mark. You're actually on Trail #5 of the Old Forge/Town of Webb Mountain Biking and Hiking Trail System, which is also called Carey Road, and is also an old railbed. Trail #5 joins the rest of the same intricate trail system that's described in Tour #1 (The Train from Thendara), which begins over 10 miles south of Eagle Bay. There are literally days' worth of riding here if that's what you're looking for.

Eagle Bay is located a mile or so southwest of Inlet on NY 28, and 10 miles northeast of Old Forge. You won't see very many distinguishing structures in Eagle Bay that will clue you in to the fact that you've arrived, except for the SuperDuper itself, which sits at the corner of NY 28 and Big Moose Road. You'll have to be creative about finding a parking spot, since there is no designated trailhead parking, and in the summertime, the supermarket parking lot tends to be pretty packed. There are, however, plenty of places to stash your car along the little road behind the SuperDuper, and in a variety of other areas you'll find if you look around a little. There is a state trail parking area just under two miles south of Eagle Bay on NY 28, where the trails to Moss, Bubb, and Sis Lakes begin (see Tour #2), and you can always find room there, but you'll lose that distance on the trail itself.

The trail follows the old railbed of the 1899 Raquette Lake Railroad (which you can also ride from Raquette Lake itself, where another 3-mile section goes south from just behind the library). As such it is mostly flat, with only a negligible grade here and there. Hybrids can handle the trail with ease and comfort.

0.0 *Set out along the trail, heading southwest, keeping NY 28 to your left.*

The trail is elevated above the road slightly (it's still set on the ballast of the original railbed), and is flat and fast. The treadway is dirt. You'll go in and out of hardwood forest.

1.6 *The trail pulls away from the road, and draws closer to it again as you go on.*

2.6 *You may be able to see Fourth Lake around here, to your left (east) depending on the season.*

3.0 *You'll come upon a map kiosk on the right-hand side of the trail that describes the Old Forge Mountain Bike Trail System.*

This is also a small, informal parking area with room for a few cars. NY 28 is just to your left. Cars are allowed on this section of what's now called Carey Road, which will surprise you, since it's such a pristine, wooded, fragile-looking area, but few people know about or take advantage of the fact. Stay alert.

The trail heads off into the woods and follows right next to a very scenic pond and wetland area on your left. There are some blue state trail markers here and there along the road.

4.6 *Pass through the wetland area and you'll see an historic signpost describing the history of the Raquette Lake Railroad, at the intersection of a foot trail that goes out to the Rondaxe Mountain Trailhead Parking Area (no bikes).*

This has been the most scenic part of the tour, and you won't be missing too much if you've decided you have had enough and want to turn around now. Very good scenery exists ahead from the

Riding the Old Forge Mountain Biking Trail System

road next to Rondaxe Lake, but you can drive there on a day when you want to explore the mountain bike trail system. Study the kiosk map for an overview, and pick up a trail system map almost anywhere in either Old Forge or Inlet.

5.0 *You will come out of the deep woods and onto a slightly improved surface.*

You're in a very sparsely populated camp area just east of Rondaxe Lake, which you may see to your right through the trees. Continue.

5.8 *At the T-intersection of Carey Road and Rondaxe Road (paved), you'll see a dirt trail or small dirt road on your right.*

A sign indicates Trail 5, Old Forge, to the right. You should take a moment to pedal .2 miles down to Rondaxe Lake now, either on the road or the trail surface, and turn around there. Excellent opportunities for extended touring on the mountain bike trail system exist here, and if you've got the time and energy, explore to the northwest. The system is well-marked, and you'll start to see signs and trail numbers immediately after crossing Rondaxe Lake, which was split off from West Lake by the railroad berm. The mountain biking and hiking trails on this (northwest) side of the trail system are flatter and more forgiving then those which originate from the Old Forge area, so if you've got kids, this is one of the best places in the region to explore creatively.

6.0 *Here on the berm at Rondaxe Lake you'll get a few good views of the lake itself and some scattered hills in the background, typical scenery here in the Fulton Chain Wild Forest.*

Turning back here to retrace your tracks to Eagle Bay will result in a very satisfying and solid tour of 12 miles, total. However, hybrid riders especially may want to consider a road ride back to their cars, and this can be accomplished by following Rondaxe Road to the left (east) from the T-intersection described at 5.8 miles. I can't recommend this option to any but the most experienced road riders, however, because NY 28 is a very busy road in the tourist season, and although there are excellent shoulders that provide good distance from traffic, people tend to go very fast here, while watching the scenery. Rondaxe Road, which road riders would have to take in order to reach NY 28, is shoulderless, though wooded and fairly quiet. A little over a mile will bring you to the Rondaxe Mountain Trailhead Parking Area, and 0.1 mile beyond that is NY 28, where you would go left to return to Eagle Bay. You don't have to go the whole way to Eagle Bay on NY 28, though. You can re-access the trail another 1.5 miles ahead (at the 3.0 milepoint described earlier).

Camping Permits and General Information

Forest Ranger Headquarters: NYSDEC, 225 North Main Street, Herkimer, NY 13350: 315-866-6330

Bike Shop

Pedals and Petals, NY 28, 176N/PO Box 390, Inlet, NY: 315-357-3281; e-mail: pedpet@telenet.net; Web site: www.tvenet.com/pedalsand-petals/

6
The Black Fly Challenge

Location: *Hamilton County, Moose River Recreation Area*
Distance: *80 miles round-trip*
Terrain: *Hilly, sandy, hard-packed dirt roads*
Rating: *Advanced if you do the entire distance; however, any level of rider can do any section.*
Maps: *The Adirondacks: West-Central Wilderness; USGS: Old Forge, Honnedaga Lake, Wakely Mountain, West Canada Lakes, Indian Lake; ADK: West Central Region*
Highlights: *One of the best places in the park for fishing, boating, camping, and other Adirondack pursuits; suitable for the entire family, with many cycling tours from beginner to intermediate ability range*

This is the infamous Black Fly Challenge, which follows the route of the annual mountain bike race of the same name. The race was conceived and popularized by Ted Christodaro, of Pedals and Petals bike shop, other local cyclists from Inlet, and the Adirondack Mountain Bike Association, and it's quickly becoming a classic. How could it not, with a name like that?

The Challenge is a wondrous, spellbinding tour that takes in the main (dirt) road of the Moose River Recreation Area as it stretches from the villages of Inlet to Indian Lake, with all sorts of possibilities for camping, fishing, boating, and combining a variety of activities for an ideal Adirondack vacation. Or you can sign up for the annual June race and undertake the BFC as a grueling distance run. The race starts at either Indian Lake or Inlet, on alternating years, and runs through the Moose River Recreation Area. Usually the really bad blackfly season is past by race time, but these flies are persistent, and there will be stragglers around for sure. The implication seems to be that you can outrun blackflies on

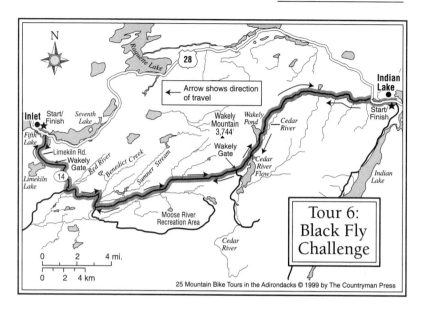

N

Racquette Lake

28

← Arrow shows direction
of travel

Inlet Start/Finish Seventh Lake

Fifth Lake

Limekiln Rd.
Wakely Gate

Limekiln Lake

14

Red River Benedict Creek Sumner Stream

Wakely Mountain 3,744' Wakely Pond

Cedar River

Wakely Gate

Cedar River Flow

Moose River Recreation Area

Cedar River

Indian Lake

Start/Finish

Indian Lake

Tour 6:
Black Fly
Challenge

0   2   4 mi.

0   2   4 km

25 Mountain Bike Tours in the Adirondacks © 1999 by The Countryman Press

a mountain bike . . . but if you slow down, they'll get you. That—and the distance—is the challenge. What better way to make time?

The Moose River Recreation Area (MRRA) is the highlight of this tour. The state handout, which you should get hold of (MRRA official map and guide), is available at most information areas, Department of Environmental Conservation (DEC) offices, and the entrance gates to the MRRA itself. It contains important information about using this area, the rules and regulations pertaining to its use, plus a usable map. Among the interesting facts noted in the guide is that the MRRA is "the largest block of remote public land in the Adirondacks readily accessible by motor vehicle." You shouldn't be discouraged by the fact that vehicles are allowed, but you should be aware of it. Weekend traffic tends to be brisk, and the speed limit isn't always heeded. Be alert, and instruct children to act accordingly. One of the drawbacks for cyclists is the dust raised by vehicles, and though the road is maintained very well, dust is ever present. But so is a slight breeze (and sometimes an outright blow), and to date, I've never had much of a cause to complain about dust—though an aerobically charged racing cyclist, keeping pace with a slow-moving car or pickup, may insist otherwise.

The dense forests, long rivers, and hundreds of ponds within the area create an unimaginably varied and exciting landscape. According to its official guide, the DEC maintains 40 miles of road, 27 miles of trails, 140 primitive tent sites, and a fire tower on Wakely Mountain within the MRRA. Forest rangers, in residence at both the Wakely and Limekiln Gates, are available to assist the public, although they prefer that you are as independent and prepared as possible and won't need their assistance other than for information.

The great thing about vehicle access to the MRRA is that you can enjoy these facilities with relatively little effort. And you can stage even longer trips into surrounding wilderness areas (on foot and by boat) that would normally prove impractical to reach. Familiarize yourself with the motor-vehicle access rules and regulations before you go. There are seasonal restrictions for RVs and two-wheel drive vehicles, and motorcycles are not permitted. The road may be closed at any given time for any number of reasons. Always double-check with a phone call (see information at end of tour).

You begin the tour at either Indian Lake or Inlet. From Indian Lake, head west out of the village on NY 28, and at 2 miles turn left onto Cedar River Road. That will take you 12 miles to the ranger headquarters at Wakely Dam. You may wish to begin the Challenge at Wakely, foregoing the pavement. If you want to do the entire trip, from Inlet to Indian Lake, here it is.

0.0   *Come out of Arrowhead Park in the village of Inlet (you can't miss it), and turn right, heading east on NY 28.*

0.2   *Pass Fifth Lake on your right.*

0.8   *Turn right on Limekiln Road (CR 14), where signs point to Limekiln State Campground and the Moose River Recreation Area.*

2.6   *Pass Limekiln State Campground.*

This would be a great place to stay if you're not interested in camping in the interior.

2.7   *Turn left into the MRRA, at Limekiln Gate.*

You must register here, particularly if you're in a vehicle. Register anyway—if anything happens to you, registration is your safety valve. Make sure you have a map with you at this point. And since you can't depend on finding safe drinking water, bring enough

The Black Fly Challenge (Moose River Recreation Area)

with you. (There is water at the Wakely Ranger's Headquarters.) Don't drink any untreated water. The road is hilly, sandy, and wide here. You begin to climb. The road levels and afterward undulates across flats and depressions.

7.5 Arrive at the first intersection.

A trail sign on the right points back toward Limekiln Gate. Straight ahead is Camping Area #1 and the trail to Rock Dam.

Go left.

Cross the Red River, heading toward Moose River (5 miles), Otter Brook (6.9 miles), and Cedar River (16.65 miles). You're heading into Camping Area #2.

11.0 Pass the trail to Mitchell Pond on your right, and cross Benedict Creek.

11.2 Cross Sumner Stream.

11.4 Arrive at a T. Turn left, following in the direction of Helldiver Pond, Lost Pond, and a series of other ponds.

Cedar River, at 13 miles, is your current destination. You have entered the Moose River Plains, an open area where you can see a number of ridges and low hills. You're now in Camping Area #3.

12.3 Pass the trail to Helldiver Pond on the right.

13.5 Pass the trail to Lost Ponds on the left.

15.4 Pass the trails to Moose River and Sly Pond on the right.

23.9 Pass the trail to Carry Lean-to.

25.1 Arrive at Wakely Gate and a camping area on Cedar River Flow.

If you want to enjoy a few days of camping, fishing, and boating along with your mountain biking, this is the place to stay. Pass through, sign out, and head east for Indian Lake Village.

25.6 Pass the trail to Wakely Mountain Observatory (elevation 3,744').

25.7 Pass Wakely Pond Outlet (a small creek).

A few brief views of wetlands and hills follow.

29.5 Seasonal dwellings begin to appear along with other signs of

civilization.

30.5 Hit the pavement. Views open up.

31.8 Pass the Northville–Lake Placid Trailhead on your left.

37.3 Turn right onto NY 28 and head into town.

37.7 Cross the Cedar River

39.6 Arrive at Indian Lake.

Congratulations. You have just completed the Black Fly Challenge!

Camping Permits and General Information

Forest Ranger Headquarters: NYSDEC, 701 South Main Street, Box 458, Northville, NY 12134: 518-863-4545

Old Forge Information/Central Adirondack Association, 315-369-6983/ Web site: www.adirondacktravel.com

Bike Shops

Pedals and Petals, NY 28, 176N, Inlet, NY: 315-357-3281; e-mail: pedpet@telenet.net.; Web site: www.tvenet.com/pedalsandpetals/

Pine's Country Store, NY 28, Box 339, Indian Lake, NY: 518-648-5212

7
Beaver Lake

Location: *Moose River Recreation Area*
Distance: *4.3 miles round-trip*
Terrain: *Gently rolling, flat*
Surface Conditions: *Grassy, dirt road*
Rating: *Beginner*
Maps: *The Adirondacks: West-Central Wilderness; USGS: Wakely Mountain; ADK: West Central Region*
Highlights: *Family tour; near good trout fishing; free camping, great boating, and many spots to hike, walk, and explore*

Beaver Lake is among the best family outings in the Moose River Recreation Area (MRRA). It's suitable to anyone with a very basic understanding of off-road bicycle handling, and it's an easy, short ride for anyone else not in the mood for rock hopping. The tour ends at the lake, where there's a close to pristine primitive campsite and not much evidence of overuse or high impact. The treadway is unusual in that it is largely flat and contains few rocks. Not a likely scenario for most of the Adirondacks! This trail, like most of the interior MRRA routes, is deep within the Moose River Wild Forest Area and will take some planning to reach and to experience safely.

From Arrowhead Park in the village of Inlet, set your odometer to zero and turn right, heading east on NY 28. At 0.2 mile, pass Fifth Lake on your right. Turn right onto Limekiln Road (CR 14), where signs point to Limekiln State Campground and the Moose River Recreation Area at 0.8 mile. At 2.6 miles, pass Limekiln State Campground, which would be a great place to stay if you're not interested in camping in the interior.

Just ahead, on your left at 2.7 miles, turn left into the MRRA, at Limekiln Gate. At 7.5 miles, you'll arrive at an intersection. There's a trail

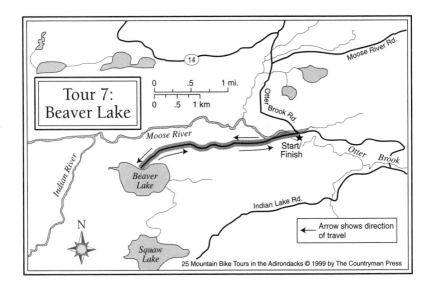

Tour 7:
Beaver Lake

Moose River Rd.

Moose River

Otter Brook Rd.

Start/
Finish

Otter Brook

Indian River

Beaver
Lake

Indian Lake Rd.

N

Squaw
Lake

Arrow shows direction
of travel

25 Mountain Bike Tours in the Adirondacks © 1999 by The Countryman Press

sign on the right, pointing back toward Limekiln Gate. Straight ahead is
Camping Area #1, and the trail to Rock Dam. Go left, across the Red
River, heading toward Moose River (5 miles), Otter Brook (6.9 miles) and
Cedar River (16.65 miles). You're heading into Camping Area #2. At 11
miles, you'll pass the trail to Mitchell Pond on your right, and shortly
afterward you cross Benedict Creek and Sumner Stream. At 11.4 miles,
you arrive at a T. There are trail signs here on the right side of the road.
Go straight here (or bear right), heading for the Beaver Lake trail. At about
12.7 miles, cross the Moose River, and just as you begin to climb away
from the river, you'll see the trail signs for Beaver Lake on the right. Turn
right here, follow the road, and park about 0.2 mile farther, on the wide
turn-around and parking area next to Otter Brook. This is the trailhead.

This is an attractive spot, remote and yet easily accessible, and there
are several rides in the area that merit camping here for a day or two. The
possibility for exploration on both the easy MRRA sand roads and legal
offshoots into wild forest environs—many of them not discussed in this
book—are endless.

Park near the barrier gate where the road widens as it crosses Otter
Brook, just before it spills into the bigger Moose River, an arrow shot
away. Downstream some distance, the Moose rages—some have called it
the best white-water run in the East—but here in the languid head-

waters, it rages not. While the Moose is substantial and moves fast, the Otter is a dull and tannic stream. But aways east, where Indian Lake Road heads for the West Canada Wilderness Area, it is wild trout water, lively and aerated with bouldered rapids and pocket water. In early spring you could camp here and feed on trout almost as easily as a Kansas camper in July could chow down on corn on the cob.

0.0 Cross the bridge over the Otter Brook.

Climb slightly, leveling off through a stretch where the Moose runs flat and silently to your right.

1.2 See if you can locate a tremendous virgin white pine on the right, with three enormous stems.

The main trunk of this tree has to be nearly 18 feet in circumference, or about 6 feet in diameter, and each trunk is about 3 feet across for a height of about 70 feet! It's one of the largest pines I've ever seen. Other ancient virgins have survived early logging operations here as well, increasing in number as you pedal and all on the right side of the trail. Towering over the ground cover of bunchberry, sorrel, and ground pine, you'll see their companions—or what's left of them—their ghostly gray dead stems leaning heavily into the second-growth forest. The trees in this transitional stand were probably spared harvesting when the understory of hardwood was logged because they were unfit for lumber at their age. At any rate, there's no even-aged understory to sustain the type, and when these big pines die, that will be the last of them. It's unlikely that you'll ever again see such a fine example of virgin white pine. (They do exist if you look around. One of the best extant examples is in the Five Ponds Wilderness Area.)

The trail now assumes an odd treadway—a tripletrack! Maybe I'm coining a new term here, but it's an accurate one. The road is actually three distinct, individual treadways, each of them soft, needle-covered dirt. The grass strip that usually appears in the middle of a rutted road has a skunk-striped singletrack right down the middle of it. You could ride three abreast, but you'd be touching elbows. The trail is flat and fast. Cruising on your middle ring, you can run at about 12 mph with ease.

2.0 Go left at a Y.

The trail dead-ends to the right in a little clearing with an old,

Typical scenery in the Moose River Recreation Area

overgrown fire ring in it. The trail you follow is grassy for a way, then turns to rock and goes steeply downhill. Though this is only a short section of downhill before it reaches the lake, the trail can be hazardous, particularly when wet. If you haven't been wearing a helmet or have been riding with it unstrapped because of the heat, get it on and strap it—or walk. On the left, partway down this section, you'll see a loon alert sign. This is a plea to those using the lake, particularly boaters, to avoid disturbing the loons. Most people don't know that disturbing a loon during nesting season may cause nest abandonment. Loons are not only a symbol of wilderness, as the sign attests, they also are *proof* of wilderness! Like the trout, they cannot live in a poisoned, crowded environment. If loons are around, it's a pretty good indicator that there's some wilderness around, too.

2.13 Arrive at the lake.

Butterflies snack on profuse white clover, and two sentinel pines mark this clean campsite. A triple-stemmed birch shades the spot, and a woodsman carved a rustic backrest out of long pine splits, which sets before the fire ring. The lake is large, and you can camp a child's stone's-throw from the water.

Return the way you came.

Camping Permits and General Information

Forest Ranger Headquarters: NYSDEC, 701 South Main Street, Box 458, Northville, NY 12134: 518-863-4545

Old Forge Information/Central Adirondack Association: 315-369-6983; Web site: www.adirondacktravel.com

Bike Shops

Pedals and Petals, NY 28, 176N, Inlet, NY: 315-357-3281; e-mail: pedpet@telenet.net.; Web site: www.tvenet.com/pedalsandpetals/

Pine's Country Store, NY 28, Box 339, Indian Lake, NY: 518-648-5212

8
Sucker Brook Bay

Location: *Hamilton County, Towns of Inlet and Raquette Lakes, Fulton Chain Wild Forest*
Distance: *6.6 miles*
Terrain: *Gently rolling*
Surface Conditions: *Sandy, dirt single- and doubletrack*
Rating: *Beginner/intermediate*
Maps: *The Adirondacks: West-Central Wilderness; ADK: West Central Region; USGS: Raquette Lake*
Highlights: *Swimming; public campground; short, fast, and easy single- and doubletrack trail*

Good swimming on the sand beaches of Upper Pond, proximity to Browns Tract Pond Public Campground and the interesting little landing at Raquette Lake, along with its modestly challenging beginner double- and singletrack trail, make Sucker Brook Bay one of the best bike trails around. From the trail's end, you can also get a swim in Raquette Lake as well as a fetching view northward toward Owls Head Mountain. This trail was only recently made accessible by improvement of the bridge over Beaver Brook, and judging by the trail's condition, it has seen little use by hikers or bikers in recent years. Because it is relatively short, its terrain even, and its obstacles few, this trail can be completed in under two hours. The particular day I chose was gray and threatening, and off in the distance thunder crashed against the hills.

The trailhead is easily reached from Eagle Bay, which is just south of Inlet and above Old Forge on NY 28. Turn west onto Uncas Road a few hundred feet north of the SuperDuper in Eagle Bay. Set your car's odometer to zero. At 2.9 miles, pass the trail to Black Bear Mountain (2 miles), and Eighth Lake (3.5 miles), which will be on your right. Keep going,

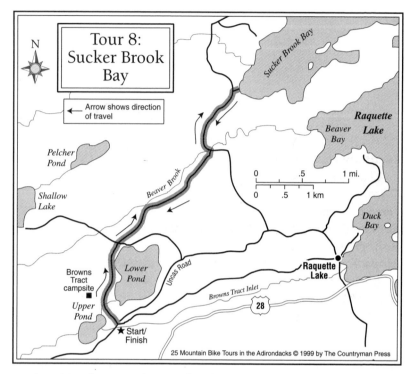

Tour 8:
Sucker Brook Bay

Arrow shows direction
of travel

Pelcher Pond

Shallow Lake

Beaver Brook

Sucker Brook Bay

Beaver Bay

Raquette Lake

Duck Bay

Browns Tract campsite

Lower Pond

Uncas Road

Raquette Lake

Upper Pond

Browns Tract Inlet

28

★ Start/ Finish

25 Mountain Bike Tours in the Adirondacks © 1999 by The Countryman Press

until at 6.1 miles you see a pond and a barrier gate on your left. This is the trail you want. Park in the available space and set out.

0.0 *Beyond the yellow barrier gate and stop sign, you'll see trail markers and a* TRAIL *sign, which offers no clue as to the identity or destination of the trail.*

The surface is a wide doubletrack. Two sand beaches are on the left, along the eastern shores of Upper Pond, which you can use. However, no camping is allowed. Follow past a white-pine forest over a sandy, leaf-covered treadway.

0.37 *You'll begin to see Lower Pond to your right.*

As you travel, you'll continue to get views of Lower Pond and will notice a few herd trails that head in the general direction of its shores.

0.61 *Pass an unnamed trail to the left.*

0.9 *Pass through an intersection.*

Raquette Lake

A trail to the left indicates Shallow Lake, and the one on the right goes to Lower Pond.

2.0 *You will encounter a blowdown area, mostly of hardwood trees, where increased levels of sunlight have caused grass and bushes to invade the trail.*

A skinny singletrack persists, and soon you are in shaded woods again. Go through a dry, bog-surrounded area as the trail becomes a skinny singletrack again.

3.2 *At a Y in a grassy area, go straight toward the lake through a promenade of small fir trees.*

The off-limits trail to the left penetrates the Pigeon Lake Wilderness Area, subsequently climbing West Mountain (elevation 2,902').

3.3 *You are now greeted by Raquette Lake and good views to the northeast.*

This is Sucker Brook Bay, which looks so much more elegant than its name would imply. A trail sign on the shore for hikers arriving by boat says WEST MOUNTAIN, 2.8 MILES. As I studied it, the sky opened. It was a hot day, so I delayed in putting on my Gore-Tex jacket. Finally when I was wet, I put it on. I hadn't bothered bringing rain pants, so my shorts got promptly soaked. The thunder and lightening were so bad that I set a record of some kind riding out over the slippery rocks and through wild freshets. As thunder and lightening seared overhead, I tucked in my chin and raced like Ichabod Crane being chased by the headless horseman. The storm seemed to be following me, and once in the safety of my car I found myself muttering, "Sucker Bay."

Along the road to Raquette Lake, which it is imperative to behold, you pass the roadside campsites of Browns Tract Pond Public Campground. The poor people encamped there must have felt as I did, hunkering under their tarps as the smoke from their smudges hung horizontally in the pines, wondering what night the movie changed in Inlet. Yet as I pulled into the hamlet (where the first post office appeared in 1889), traveling the same road that Sir John Johnson did as he fled to Canada, I could see a lick of salmon pink in the western sky, and I swear I could smell the cedar siding of the great camps across the lake.

Camping Permits and General Information:

Forest Ranger Headquarters: NYSDEC, 701 South Main Street, Box 458, Northville, NY 12134: 518-863-4545

Old Forge Information/Central Adirondack Association: 315-369-6983; Web site: www.adirondacktravel.com

Bike Shops

Pedals and Petals, NY 28, 176N, Inlet, NY: 315-357-3281; e-mail: pedpet@telenet.net; Web site: www.tvenet.com/pedalsandpetals/

Pine's Country Store, NY 28, Box 339, Indian Lake, NY: 518-648-5212

9

Beaver River Bike and Boat Tour

Location: Herkimer County, Town of Webb, Independence River Wild Forest

Distance: Approximately 20 miles, many options

Terrain: Flat to slightly hilly

Surface Conditions: Hard to loose sand and dirt roads

Rating: Intermediate

Maps: The Adirondacks: West-Central Wilderness; USGS: Stillwater, Beaver River

Highlights: The water taxi on Stillwater Reservoir (9 miles—call ahead for schedule), visiting a town with no access roads; swimming and fishing; wilderness flavor; historical interest. Overnight accommodations available at the Beaver River Hotel or the Norridgewock Resort.

Inevitably, someone will ask me the tantalizing question, "So what's your favorite tour in the entire book?" Here's your answer: This is a trip you'll enjoy even if you don't take your bike. And as far as bike tours go, this is the most intriguing, fun, and off-beat ride around. It's not as out-of-the-way as you may have been told when you first muttered the word "Stillwater" to your friends, but it is a good 40-minute drive west of Eagle Bay (which is north of Old Forge) over a long and dusty dirt road into one of the wildest realms of the Adirondacks. It's all part of the adventure! You'll never forget the tiny, friendly town of Beaver River (pop. 85), the large and many islanded Stillwater Reservoir with its hundred miles of shoreline, and the easy, sandy, 20 miles of off-road riding you can enjoy, going through town and the adjoining fens and open vistas of the Independence River Wild Forest. Luckily for the cyclist, this forest just missed—by the width of one railbed—being classified as a state forest preserve wilderness area.

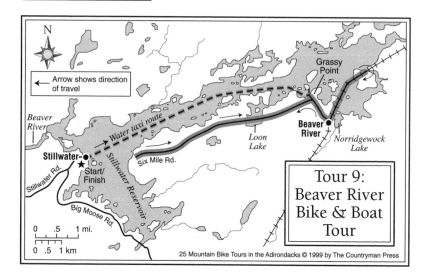

Map labels: N — Arrow shows direction of travel — Grassy Point — Beaver River — Water taxi route — Loon Lake — Beaver River — Norridgewock Lake — Stillwater — Start/Finish — Six Mile Rd. — Stillwater Rd. — Stillwater Rd. — Stillwater Reservoir — Big Moose Rd. — 0 .5 1 mi. — 0 .5 1 km

Tour 9: Beaver River Bike & Boat Tour

25 Mountain Bike Tours in the Adirondacks © 1999 by The Countryman Press

   This ride begins by boat at Stillwater Landing, your departure point as well as the location of a general store, restaurant, marina, public boat launch, and Department of Environmental Conservation (DEC) ranger headquarters. You can reach the area from Lowville by turning easterly off NY 12 in the center of the village, onto River Street, which becomes Number Four Road. Follow 5 miles into Bushes Landing. Bear left, and continue 9 miles to the hamlet of Number Four. Turn right onto Stillwater Road, and follow that 8.5 miles to Stillwater Reservoir.

   If you're coming from NY 28, first find Big Moose Road, which goes west from Eagle Bay. (Eagle Bay, which is just under 2 miles south of Inlet, is roughly equidistant between Raquette Lake to the north and Old Forge to the south, on NY 28.) Turn west (it's the only way you can turn) on Big Moose Road, where signs indicate Stillwater at 18 miles. Traveling over a paved road at this point, you're passing through the Fulton Chain Wild Forest environs, and you'll see several trailheads, including, on your left at 2 miles, the Moss Lake trail system (see chapter 2). Pass Big Moose Lake, of which you'll have only scant views, and turn left at a Y at 5.9 miles (Glenmore Corner). At 7.7 miles, pass the old Big Moose Station (a stop on the Adirondack Scenic Railroad), and the road turns to dirt. Some people recommend that you ride this section of road to Stillwater on your bike, which isn't a bad idea sometimes. But it tends to be very, very dusty, and traffic—in spite of the loose surface, hills, and curves—goes pretty fast, often towing fishtailing boats or campers, adding to the dust problem. This is a very busy area during the peak season, and the DEC has been managing camping very carefully. Water quality, ground impact from heavy camping, and increased traffic has caused the area to lose some of its remote quality. Time your trip to avoid the masses.

Until you reach the southeast bay of Stillwater Reservoir, in the vicinity of Stillwater Mountain (trail elevation 2,264'), there are no great views, and there are much better places to ride in the area without contending with traffic (like, where you're going). If you want to ride this road, pick a weekday off-season after a rainstorm.

At 17.5 miles, turn right and arrive at the landing at 18 miles, as promised. There's plenty of activity here on a weekend, plus a lot of parking. There's also a state ranger, who can answer questions and assign designated campsites, should you have your own boat or wish to rent one. Call up the water taxi from the public phone, and pack your bags. Just to be sure, call ahead from Old Forge or Eagle Bay for schedules and fares. The ads say the boat is "on call any time, daily, except Wednesdays, from July 1." (Off-season the taxi runs on an as-needed basis.) Since the cost is per boatload, it helps to have several people share the cost. You may be able to connect with other passengers at each end of the trip. The tourist information office in Old Forge has phones and phone numbers to help with your planning. Pack according to your plans, but don't forget rain gear, insect repellent, and tools (don't expect to find a bike shop). And unless you are an ironperson, don't plan to ride out on the railroad tracks back to Big Moose Station. It's a 9-mile walk.

Someday, in the near future, the railroad may come to Beaver River, which will make this an even more interesting trip. For now, your boat ride to Grassy Point Landing, where you will begin the tour, is a scenic 20-minute, 9-mile boat ride.

0.0 *Upon your arrival at Grassy Point, depart the water taxi, and head southeast—the only direction you can go—toward town.*

0.1 *Pass the Colvin Rock Trail (legal, unresearched) on your left.*

0.2 *Pass Six Mile Road on your right.*

You'll return to ride this road later on. (Corridor 8 snowmobile signs abound here; this is a popular destination for sledders, who either ride the railbeds or come across the lake.) If you find that

Stillwater Landing

the sections of soft sand here are giving you problems, remember to keep your weight back over your seat, and try letting a little air out of your tires. Slicks and baldies work best on sand. Hybrids will have the most trouble. Fortunately, deep sand is mostly limited to this particular stretch of road.

Keep going straight.

You'll begin to see camps as you enter the town "limits" (there are about 100 camps in all) and will pass the hotel on your right, coming upon the railroad tracks. You'll see the Norridgewock Resort in front of you. The resort belongs to the Thompson family, who've been in residence here since 1918. Stop and say hello, relax (after all, you've come a half mile), and catch up on the local news. Both the resort and the hotel welcome overnight guests. And don't forget you can camp anywhere in the forest preserve, provided you follow the rules.

Turn left and follow the tracks (abandoned until future notice) out to Big Culvert.

This is a rather fancy name for a diminutive pipe between a large bay and Norridgewock Lake. This and the causeway that stretches out to the northeast are the most scenic spots in town.

1.4 *Arrive at the culvert, which is shown on the map in the "Welcome Aboard the Norridgewock Riverboat" handout (just ask any member of the Thompson clan).*

The riverboat provides intimate tours around Stillwater Reservoir, which is also called Beaver River Flow. We hung around and watched as kids pulled in bullheads here. These little catfish make fine eating and are popular fare among Adirondackers in general. They're plentiful though small, bite eagerly on worms, and have a delicate, reddish flesh. Elsewhere in the reservoir—in itself a popular smallmouth bass fishery—are brown trout, splake (a cross between a brook, or speckled trout, and a lake trout), and yellow perch.

Immediately across the culvert, take the skinny singletrack running along the built-up berm causeway. Follow this trail as far as you can before foliage and profuse ballast stone causes you enough trouble to call it quits.

The scenery here is phenomenal. The tracks continue to Brandreth, Keepawa, Partlow, and finally to Tupper Lake, its right-of-way traversing private as well as state lands. The berm is decked with wild columbines, and loons trill indignant tremolos as the ballast stones ching like wind chimes in your spokes. Warm winds blowing in from the Five Ponds Wilderness keep the flies at bay as you gaze among the low hills and wetlands between you and Little Rapids, just up the tracks. To your southeast lies a beautiful wasteland, a hunk of Forever Wild called the Pigeon Lake Wilderness—a swath of humpy, buggy, mind-boggling backland that you could walk for 20 miles across without encountering road, trail, or tenant, all the way to Raquette Lake. But for one private road, you could double that distance, arriving in Long Lake.

1.4 *Return to the way you came, and take a left just before you reach the Norridegwock Resort (a modest and appealing edifice). Turn left on this road and cross a bridge.*

Here you'll encounter a forest preserve centennial monument to Verplank Colvin, the Adirondacks' first surveyor, a founder of the state forest preserve, and one of the few Adirondack personalities to escape history with his reputation still intact. You can explore, minimally, the roads that emanate from both sides of Norridgewock Lake, but the distances are minuscule. When you find your way back to the tracks, you should have accumulated a distance of 3 or 4 miles. Reset to zero, and head for Six Mile Road (back toward the boat landing). This part of the trip is visually anticlimactic, but it's better biking.

0.0 *Head west, back toward the boat landing.*

0.6 *Go left on Six Mile Road.*

This is a deep forest ride, with limited views. It's hilly to begin with and undulating thereafter.

2.5 *Cross the swamplands around Loon Lake, which is really a bay.*

This is the last of the scenery until you reach the landing, which isn't really a landing but a dead-end. The rest of the ride is woods, mostly deciduous, over ancient cedar corduroy in some places, remnants of the days when French and Indian soldiers engaged in warfare against the British. "Corduroying" a trail is a method of laying down small trees, usually cedar, to form a durable treadway for foot and wagon use.

6.0 *The road ends with a right turn down to the water's edge.*

It's difficult to be retrieved here by the taxi, although we did it by special arrangement, wading chest-deep to hand our bikes into the boat. For most, it's probably a better idea to turn around and pick up the trail again at Grassy Point. Make arrangements at the resort before riding Six Mile Road, or you may miss the boat altogether. Let's just hope it's not the last taxi ride of the year. There's a rumor afoot that this is how the town of Beaver River builds its population. In any event, you may not *want* to leave this forest Shangri La for "civilization."

Camping Permits and General Information:

Forest Ranger Headquarters: NYSDEC, 225 North Main Street, Herkimer, NY 13350: 315-866-6330

Old Forge Information/Central Adirondack Association: 315-369-6983; Web site: www.adirondacktravel.com

Bike Shops

Pedals and Petals, NY 28, 176N, Inlet, NY: 315-357-3281; e-mail: pedpet@telenet.net; Web site: www.tvenet.com/pedalsandpetals/

Pine's Country Store, NY 28, Box 339, Indian Lake, NY: 518-648-5212

Sporting Proposition, Main Street, Old Forge, NY: 315-369-6188

10
Uncas Road, Raquette Lake Loop

Location: Hamilton County, Moose River Plains Wild Forest, Towns of Inlet and Long Lake
Terrain: Gently rolling to hilly
Distance: Total 19.2 miles in 3.7-mile, 6.0-mile, and 9.5-mile individually ridable sections
Surface Conditions: Dirt roads, singletrack
Rating: Advanced/Expert
Maps: The Adirondacks: West-Central Wilderness; USGS: Raquette Lake, Wakely Mountain; ADK: West Cental Region
Highlights: Raquette Lake village; the Adirondack Great Camp Sagamore; camping in nearby state campgrounds

Bound for infamy, this tour combines the stunning scenery of Raquette Lake and the simple, old-fashioned mood of its tiny village with a look at Sagamore, an Adirondack Great Camp, a ride through two state campgrounds, and miles of great dirt road and singletrack cycling.

In all of the mountain biking literature and on most of the maps I have found to date (except the 7.5 x 15-minute series USGS), Uncas Road is not described adequately for safe or efficient navigation. But after getting lost (or turned around) and retracing my steps on several occasions, here is a fail-safe set of directions for enjoying this fascinating and demanding ride. The tour can be conveniently broken down into three lesser tours or handled as an all-day odyssey for which you should be *flawlessly* prepared. You'll be venturing into sections of the Moose River Plains Wild Forest, on the edges of the Blue Ridge Wilderness Area, and you need to take precautions accordingly; be sure to bring adequate food, water, tools, etc.

This tour is best treated as an all-day ride for even the accomplished

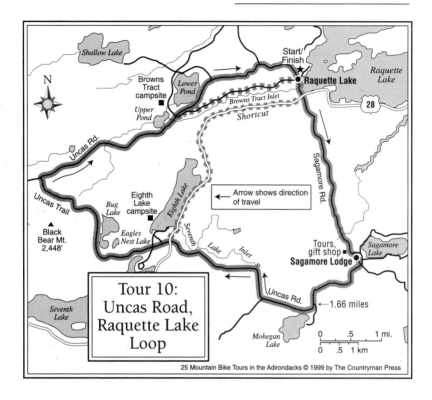

Tour 10:
Uncas Road,
Raquette Lake
Loop

25 Mountain Bike Tours in the Adirondacks © 1999 by The Countryman Press

rider, who may want to stop at both Sagamore as well as Raquette Lake village. Those who desire a less demanding itinerary can break down the ride into segments, bearing in mind the respective terrain of each piece, which will be made evident as the tour unfolds.

It's perhaps most convenient to begin at Raquette Lake village, which is just 0.3 mile north on Uncas Road from NY 28 at approximately 10 miles east of Inlet and 14 miles west of Blue Mountain Lake. Both Eighth Lake and Browns Tract Pond Public Campgrounds are ideal starting places, but you've got to go through Raquette Lake in any event.

You may find yourself asking just where Raquette Lake village really is as you're sitting right in the middle of it. This is a no-frills village at first glance—no kitschy gift shops or soft-serve ice cream stands—but you'll soon discover the secrets and nuances of a place that's been a jumping off point to the heart of the Adirondacks since Sir John Johnson and his band of Mohawk Indians encamped on its shores, leaving their snowshoes ("raquettes") behind with the spring thaw, thus giving the lake its name. Though some will smirk at this romantic notion, which has as its basis only the French translation for snowshoe, tour guides and history buffs are still fond of pointing out the very stand of pines marking the site where the raquettes were abandoned, so laying claim to a slice of French and Indian War history that James Fenimore Cooper elevated to mythical status in *Last of the Mohicans* (1826). Enter Uncas, who was himself that singular last Mohican: a good, uncorrupted natural man who perished while trying to save Cora Munro from the evil Huron, Magua. You won't find a Magua Road around here.

Raquette Lake has a couple of churches and only one bar, which says something else about the place. And it has a huge general store, the (very unassuming) Raquette Lake Supply Company, which sells almost everything for the camp-bound and incidental traveler, including ice cream cones. You'll also find gas, bait, boat rentals, a library, a boat launch and dock, and a caboose commemorating the Raquette Lake Railroad, where J.P. Morgan and his ilk once kept a few locomotives and private cars ready to go ("up to steam") at all times. The little blinking railroad lights at the makeshift crossing will continue blinking in perpetuity, I am told. Here you will also find the tour boat *W.W. Durant*, named for the erstwhile resident and preeminent American architect (and son of the Union Pacific founder) who built Sagamore. The boat ride is highly recommended; it features cruise and dine tours, buffets, moonlight cruises, champagne brunches, and weddings. The captain, a lifelong resident of Raquette Lake, maintains a running live dialogue on the history and development of the area.

To get on with the ride from Raquette Lake, stash your car in any of the evident lots, and, starting from the boat launch area, face your bicycle south toward NY 28 and Sagamore Road, which you'll see on the map. This section of road to Sagamore is suitable to hybrids and even sturdy touring bikes, but it is dirt, so forget those skinny velo tires. Pedal across the scenic Browns Tract Inlet, and stop at the intersection of NY 28. A water fountain is on your left here, and an historic plaque is on your right.

0.0 Head straight across NY 28 onto Sagamore Road, which is marked DEAD END.

This is a fast-cruising, dirt-surfaced road that passes a few creeks and trailheads.

3.5 *Bear right at the Sagamore sign, and cross its outlet.*

The lefthand turn goes down to the lake, and from that point foot trails enter the forest preserve.

3.7 *Opposite a service building that houses Sagamore's gift shop and information center (the main camp complex is on the lake) is a parking area.*

Park here if you're planning to tour the facility (several tours run daily, and you must register and pay a fee). Inquire as to where to lock up your bike. Sagamore is not like a regular hotel. It invites guests but only on a three-day-minimum-stay basis, during which time heritage and other educational and recreational residential programs are offered. These include such things as kayak building, plant ecology, Great Camps weekends, music and dance, and—alas, recently—mountain biking! Sagamore also rents mountain bikes and provides leaders for their many interpretive and educational outings. Keep going after your stop at the gift shop, or your Great Camp tour, if you want to ride the most demanding singletrack section of this tour.

Reset to zero. Accuracy is important now.

0.0 *Go straight on the dirt road, leaving the gift shop on your left.*

0.18 *Turn right at a Y.*

This road is gated off and has a forbidding-looking NO UNAUTHO-RIZED VEHICLES sign posted, but it's state land. Go under or around the gate, and you'll see friendly state forest preserve signs on the trees. Kamp Kill Kare, to the left at this Y, was built on W.W. Durant's former holdings, and Uncas, ahead on (private) Mohegan Lake, was first J.P. Morgan's place and later Alfred G. Vanderbilt's. Climb enviously up a long hill.

1.66 *Bear right onto a lesser dirt road, where at this time a brown-and-yellow trail arrow is nailed precariously to a sapling.*

This becomes an easy, pleasant riding surface.

1.72 *About 150 feet in, pass through a barrier gate. Cruise easily.*

2.63 *This is the critical spot. Start paying close attention, or you're apt to go miles out of your way, dead-ending at a private hunting camp.*

The Adirondack Great Camp Sagamore's bookshop

You're crossing a north (right)-flowing creek over a short plank bridge. This creek is apparently nameless, though it's the same watershed that feeds South Inlet and Raquette Lake. Get off your bike here, and walk ahead, watching carefully to your right until, still in view of the bridge, Uncas "Road" goes off into the woods. This is not a grandiose, full-scale road as most maps and trail descriptions would lead you to believe but a cryptic little single-track that only tries to emulate a road farther downhill—and as a result of forest invasion and erosion, never quite succeeds. A yellow trail arrow on the left is directly opposite the trail, and a deceptively vague homemade plaque near it sports the chiseled scrawl, 8TH LAKE-RT 28. Happily employed at the cranks of his mountain bike, Uncas himself could have missed this one.

Turn right onto this skinny little trail, which soon widens enough to become self-guiding.

2.83 Cross a creek.

3.0   At a Y, bear right.

The left fork, a marked snowmobile trail that is inaccurately shown on every map I've ever seen as a continuation of the trail through the previously mentioned private hunting camp, is the correct (but not recommended) location of the trail to Buck Creek and NY 28 at benchmark 1,843' alongside Seventh Lake. A spur from the camps to the trail or a later rerouting may be the reason for this apparent inaccuracy. It starts out looking good, but forest rangers say it's presently full of 4-inch blowdowns. Your own treadway is not all that great, a sometimes mired and eroded surface of ups and downs, but it's not bad either, and is clear of obstacles. Sagamore's staff is planning to improve the trail's condition and markings. Beyond this point, follow a series of fast downhills resplendent with rock hops and grassed-over bumps.

4.9 *Cross a feeder creek of Seventh Lake Inlet, where the tiny bridge and culvert are washed out.*

5.55 *Cross Seventh Lake Inlet, where the culvert is also out.*

Both it and the above washout can be forded with dry feet (if you're not already soaked).

6.0 *Arrive at NY 28 and go right, making a left within a hundred or so feet into the entrance of Eighth Lake Public Campground.*

At this point, should you choose to shun the (easier) 3.5 mile Bug Lake section of the tour, Raquette Lake is 4.6 miles east on NY 28, where you crossed onto Sagamore Road. The shoulder is good.

Enter through the main gate and proceed straight into the campsite toward sites #s 72–121.

Just before the lefthand turn into the #72–121 loop, you'll see a trail arrow (NYS yellow on brown). Set your odometer at the tiny little trailhead, which is not identified. This is the Bug Lake–Black Bear Mountain Trailhead, shown on the map as Uncas Trail.

0.0 *Head into the woods, immediately crossing Seventh Lake outlet on a wide plank bridge.*

Climb easily on a smoothish doubletrack.

0.55 *At a Y, bear left, crossing the outlet creek from Eagles Nest and Bug Lakes.*

A spur trail heads to Eagles Nest Lake on the right before the bridge. The trail is fast and beautiful as you ride next to Bug Lake for about a mile.

2.5 *Cross a plank bridge over the inlet of Browns Tract Ponds, and climb.*

2.7 *Go straight past the trail to Black Bear Mountain (elevation 2,448').Descend.*

3.5 *Arrive at Uncas Road (dirt), and go right toward Raquette Lake.*

6.5 *Pass Upper Pond on your left (where the trail leaves for the Sucker Brook Bay Tour), and ride on, passing through the Browns Tract Public Campground area (sites are situated along the road next to Lower Pond).*

An alternate, easier, and more pleasant route than the road to Raquette Lake begins opposite Upper Pond (near where the trail departs for Sucker Bay) on the right. This is the old railroad bed, which brings you out to Raquette Lake directly.

9.5 *Arrive in Raquette Lake.*

Camping Permits and General Information:

Forest Ranger Headquarters: NYSDEC, 701 South Main Street, Box 458, Northville, NY 12134: 518-863-4545

Old Forge Information/Central Adirondack Association: 315-369 6983; Web site: www.adirondacktravel.com

Bike Shops

Pedals and Petals, NY 28, 176N, Inlet, NY: 315-357-3281; e-mail: pedpet@telenet.net; Web site: www.tvenet.com/pedalsandpetals/

Pine's Country Store, NY 28, Box 339, Indian Lake, NY: 518-648-5212

Sporting Proposition, Main Street, Old Forge, NY: 315-369-6188

II. NORTHWEST LAKES

11
Otter Hollow and Fish Creek Loops

Location: *Franklin County, Town of Santa Clara, Fish Creek Pond/Rollins Pond Public Campgrounds*
Distance: *13.1-mile loop, 8.7-mile loop*
Terrain: *Singletrack trails with short, easy hills and long, winding flats in lakeside and deep forest setting*
Surface Conditions: *Dirt, roots, and rocks; mud and stream crossings (depending on trail maintenance); possible blowdowns*
Rating: *Intermediate/advanced*
Maps: *Adirondack Canoe Map; USGS: St. Regis; campsite handout map; ADK: Northern Region*
Highlights: *Proximity to public campgrounds at Fish Creek Pond/Rollins Pond as well as primitive sites in Floodwood Recreation Area along Floodwood Road; direct access to St. Regis Canoe Area, Upper Saranac Lake, and numerous ponds with easy-access free camping.*

The loops described here are for the intermediate to advanced rider and traverse locally popular trails that are getting increasing attention from visiting ATBers. The system can be accessed from the two adjoining state campgrounds or from Floodwood Road. For the convenience of those staying at either Fish Creek Pond or Rollins Pond campgrounds, directions are given from within the campgrounds themselves. Free primitive campsites can be found along Floodwood Road and are good for those of a fast-moving crowd who want to save the campground fee to put toward lunch or gas (there are dozens of similar sites in the area; just ask around). However, it is ill-advised to leave any personal belongings like tents and boats at these unsupervised areas. Pack everything up before departing. Competition for these sites is fierce on weekends, during the month of August in particular.

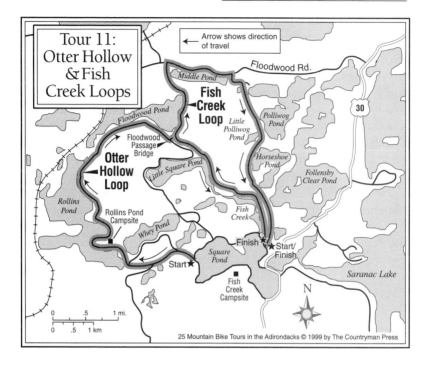

Tour 11:
Otter Hollow
& Fish
Creek Loops

Arrow shows direction
of travel

Floodwood Rd.

Middle Pond

**Fish
Creek
Loop**

Floodwood Pond

*Little
Polliwog
Pond*

*Polliwog
Pond*

30

Floodwood
Passage
Bridge

**Otter
Hollow
Loop**

Little Square Pond

*Horseshoe
Pond*

*Follensby
Clear Pond*

*Rollins
Pond*

Rollins Pond
Campsite

*Fish
Creek*

Whey Pond

Finish ★ Start/
★ Finish

Start ★

*Square
Pond*

Fish
Creek
Campsite

N

Saranac Lake

0   .5   1 mi.

0   .5   1 km

25 Mountain Bike Tours in the Adirondacks © 1999 by The Countryman Press

Fish Creek/Rollins Pond Public Campgrounds lie east of Tupper Lake on NY 30. To reach it from the Northway (I-87), take Exit 30 onto NY 9 North, and follow to NY 73 North to Lake Placid. Take NY 85 north through Saranac Lake to NY 186 West; then follow NY 30 South for 9 miles to the campground entrance. For those who plan to stage from Floodwood Road, it can be found about 3.4 miles north of the campground on NY 30, adjacent to the golf course (turn left out of the campground's main entrance onto NY 30, then left again onto Floodwood Road). Primitive sites begin about a mile down the road, along the edge of Polliwog Pond, and continue to Middle Pond, and some are on no pond at all but simply alongside the road in densely wooded areas. To access the trail system discussed here, you can either ride through the main gate of the campground or begin from a point on the trail along Floodwood Road (see text for details). The two trails that ingress from Floodwood Road can be found a mile apart on the south side, roughly at each end of Middle Pond. A little reconnoitering will uncover these trails, which are currently marked only with snowmobile discs of varying color and condition.

The state of mountain biking in this area introduces questions of management that have not been adequately addressed, especially as regards some sections of the Otter Hollow Loop, which have become badly impacted but are nonetheless still open. It is of use to the proactive among us to see the type of impact that trails in proximity to intensive public use areas must endure and how, over time, the character of those trails is changed forever under the influence of a single user group. While it is true that these trails are also used enthusiastically by hikers, the patterns of erosion you may see on the wet swales and sidehills around Square Pond and Fish Creek are markedly those borne of the fat-tire crowd. Other sections of this trail evidently can, purely by coincidence, withstand the present carrying capacity. It is my feeling that trail segments that have proven less resistant to the current strain of use patterns should be temporarily closed for recovery and reevaluation. Here we see firsthand the shortcomings of such blanket policies as our "Wild Forest Only and Anywhere" mandate for bikes, and we ponder the potential for individual trail evaluation and use designation. I have not included these specific sections of trail and have modified traditional descriptions of the loops to avoid them. But if you do decide to ride them, I would ask you to walk the evident areas rather than contribute to their present levels of overuse and unconscious abuse—a practice that holds true for any trail.

Fish Creek Loop

0.0 Go through the main gate of the Fish Creek Pond/Rollins Pond Public Campground, and turn right, heading into the campsite area on the paved access road.

You may want to park in the day-use area, which is 0.2 mile to the left as you come through the entrance. This little convenience will cost you $5 and give you access to the beach, showers, etc.

0.2 Watch carefully until opposite site #23, on your right, where you'll see a sign for Fish Creek Loop, Rollins Pond Campground, etc. Follow this trail toward campsites C-17, C-1, and C-7.

The exact treadway is unclear for a moment, but all the little paths will quickly funnel you onto a red-marked snowmobile trail near site C-2 and again near site C-6. Head north, away from the road, when you find the trail. This singletrack section is rooty, and front suspension will prove most welcome. Marking is good and the trail is self-guiding.

0.9 *Go straight through the intersection at the canoe carry between Follensby Clear Pond and Fish Creek, following the trail that runs along the edge of Fish Creek, which is not yet clearly visible on your left.*

The roots persist. There are some huge hemlocks here. Incidentally, canoe carries in this area can be ridden since they are not "sanctioned" canoe areas, such as the St. Regis Canoe Area, which do not allow bikes.

2.4 *You pass a couple of very attractive primitive tenting sites on your left, on Little Square Pond at its confluence with Floodwood Passage Creek.*

The trail has become less rooty. If you're contemplating camping, this is the place to do it.

3.0 *Reaching an intersection, you'll see trail signs and Floodwood Passage Bridge to your left. Bear right, following the sign to* FLOODWOOD ROAD, 1.5M

3.1 *At a campsite next to Floodwood Pond, bear right, keeping the pond on your left.*

3.9 *At a T, where a canoe carry goes left (southwest) toward Floodwood Pond, go right, uphill.*

Cross some poorly constructed informal log bridges that need help. You'll see snowmobile markers and yellow canoe carry discs through here.

4.0 *Turn left at a T; then a spur to the right goes down to Middle Pond.*

4.3 *Cross a little bridge through a wetland. The trail is good.*

4.6 *Come out on Floodwood Road, and turn right.*

The trail is well marked from the road but not identified except as a snowmobile trail. Ride next to Middle Pond on your right.

5.6 *Turn right into the woods again, where the trail is only marked as a snowmobile trail.*

5.7 *Turn left at a T (canoe carry). The trail is excellent—flat, fast, and in good condition.*

5.9 *Turn right at a point where the canoe carry continues ahead (left) on a narrow path toward Polliwog Pond.*

Good views of the lake soon appear on your left.

6.9 *Go straight through an intersection of the trail and a canoe carry between Polliwog and Little Polliwog Ponds.*

7.1 *Come down a short hill and ford a small stream where the bridge has recently been awash.*

You may have to get wet here. Be sure to hoist your bike high enough so that water doesn't get into the bottom bracket and the bearings. Travel along next to Horseshoe Pond.

8.9 *Pass the canoe carry you came through at 0.9 mile (Follensby Clear Pond to Fish Creek). Go straight, uphill.*

9.8 *Come out of the woods next to campsite C-2, and turn left to the main campsite entrance.*

13.1 *Arrive at the campsite entrance (and go 0.2 mile farther to the day-use parking area if you parked there).*

Otter Hollow Loop

Come through the main campsite entrance, and follow the signs to Rollins Pond on the main campsite access road. If you've elected to pay the modest day-use fee, you can drive into Rollins Pond and park at the fisherman's access parking area or at some other location acceptable to park officials.

0.0 *Turn right at a Y toward Rollins Pond Campground, just opposite site #134 of Fish Creek Pond campsite.*

0.2 *Pass the shower building.*

0.9 *Enter the Rollins Pond main gate. Proceed straight to the end of this road.*

Riding in Fish Creek Ponds State Campground

3.9 The trail moves into the woods at site #257 (there's a bathroom).

3.9 At the apex of this hairpin turn-around, you'll see signs that identify the trail to Floodwood Passage and Fish Creek Campground. Follow the trail into the woods, east of Rollins Pond and Floodwood Pond.

This is a singletrack trail that, judging by its condition, receives the least use of all the campsite trails. The area is sensitive, however, and because of the soft soils, you should avoid using this trail in wet periods.

4.5 *Cross a small wooden bridge. The trail becomes rough in spots, and your progress won't be much better than walking speed.*

5.0 *A few nice-looking campsites appear to the left on the shore of Floodwood Pond.*

5.3 *Cross a wooden bridge.*

5.7 *Arrive at Floodwood Passage Bridge, and go left, crossing it. Turn right, and head for Fish Creek Pond Campground, which is signed at 2 miles (it's actually a bit more).*

Follow the trail back to the campsite road. You will take a rooty singletrack trail and pass through the Follensby Clear Pond/Fish Creek Canoe Carry.

8.5 *Emerge from the woods at site #C-6, just across the campsite access road from site #23. Go left to reach the main gate and day-use parking area. Go right if you started at campsite #134, or the fisherman's access parking area.*

For more detail on the section of trail from Floodwood Passage Bridge to the campsite access road at site #23, see the beginning of the Fish Creek Loop Tour.

8.7 *Arrive back at the main entrance to Fish Creek Pond Public Campground.*

Camping Permits and General Information

Forest Ranger Headquarters: NYSDEC, Route 86, Box 296, Ray Brook, NY 12977-0296: 518-897-1200

Bike Shops:

Barkeater Bike Shop, 49 Main Street, Saranac Lake, NY: 518-891-5207; 1-800-254-5207

World Cup Ski, Board, and Bike, 68 Park Street, Tupper Lake, NY: 518-359-9481; e-mail: worldcup@tvenet.com

12
Deer Pond Loop

Location: *Franklin County, Town of Altamont, Saranac Lakes Wild Forest*
Distance: *7.85 miles*
Terrain: *Choice of flat, in-out singletrack/doubletrack route or moderately difficult technical trail*
Surface: *Tar, compacted dirt, and sandy loam*
Rating: *Intermediate/advanced*
Maps: *The Adirondacks: Northwest Lakes; Adirondack Canoe Map; USGS: Tupper Lake, Upper Saranac Lake; ADK: Northern Region*
Highlights: *Ponds, wetlands, and forest character with swimming at Deer Pond; proximity to Fish Creeks Pond and Rollins Pond Public Campground and Public Day-Use Areas.*

It wasn't my day to ride Deer Pond, but there I was, right in front of the trailhead, stopping to check my maps on the way to ride the epic 28-mile Dumas out of Horseshoe Lake (see Tour #14). I had to save my strength. Maybe from the parking lot I could get a peek at the trail. It looked good. Could I do them both in a day? As I pulled on my Lycra and flailed at the hordes of mosquitoes that followed me back into my van, a colorful mountain biker decked out in Team Casio stuff and mounted on a performance bike with those nice Spinergy wheels warmed down with a few tight, lazy circles near the trailhead. Before I could talk to him (and I sure couldn't catch him), he sped south on NY 30. I didn't know it at the time, but I was soon to discover that the fellow in question was none other than World Cup champion mountain bike downhiller Mike Sabin, owner of World Cup Ski, Board, and Bike Shop in Tupper Lake. I found myself hoping that the trails here weren't as demanding as Mike made them look like they were. I didn't want to sweat too much—not this early, with a 30-mile ride scheduled for the same day.

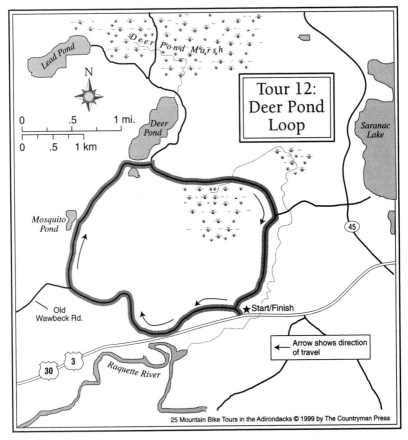

Tour 12:
Deer Pond
Loop

Arrow shows direction
of travel

25 Mountain Bike Tours in the Adirondacks © 1999 by The Countryman Press

The trailhead, which is an easy ride from Fish Creek Pond Public Campground, is between the villages of Tupper and Saranac Lake on NY 30/NY 3. There's not a huge parking space, so on a weekend you might have to look around. Boat launches for the Raquette River are both north and south of the trailhead within easy cycling distance. Find the trailhead about 0.5 mile west of the intersections of NY 30 and NY 3, some 16 miles west of Saranac Lake. A big fancy trailhead sign here says SARANAC LAKES WILD FOREST CROSS COUNTRY SKI TRAILS TO DEER POND AND RT 30 AT BULL POINT. The signage degenerates beyond this point. Pull in and park.

I sprayed myself with Natrapel and hoisted my mock-hybrid Gary Fisher Aquila off the rack. Last season I'd equipped the bike with slick, on-off road tires. By all accounts, Deer Pond is publicized as a low-end, intermediate-to-advanced trail, and my back needed a break from the low bars and aggressive geometry of my Y-bike. I was finding that the slicks gave me plenty of extra speed on the hardpack but were poor if not hazardous on wet, cornering, crumbly, steep, and especially muddy terrain. It was a bright, dry, sunny day, and I anticipated a few miles of old road and an easy backcountry sightseeing jaunt. And that's an accurate summation of this otherwise deep-woods, remotely located trail that reaches far into the Saranac Lakes Wild Forest area, traversing wetlands and skirting a few bulky hills in the 1,800' class, featuring a pair of clean, scenic ponds. It's a trail that's suited to hybrids (although fat tires are preferable), and it's user-friendly to a wide range of ability groups, including spirited, seasoned younger riders who don't whine excessively. It's not a good trail for any sort of tag-a-long or baby carrier, however. And helmets are a must.

0.0 *Go through the barrier gate, and ride along a wide tar road that is steadily being reclaimed by nature.*

0.1 *On your right, you'll pass a little woods road covered in pine needles, then shortly after that, another one. Continue straight.*

If you're an entry-level rider, have kids with you, or are just in the mood for an easy outing, you should turn right here, heeding the map and trail description that follows backward, coming back out from Deer Pond the way you came in. It's the easy way to go, and you still get to Deer Pond. If you want a great ride with children of any ability, the trail into the wetland bridge and back (2.5-mile round-trip) is as much fun as any trail in the area, and it's dead flat.

The next 2.4 miles of tar are easy.

Ride along through a pleasant wooded setting, more or less paralleling NY 30, which you can't see or hear for the most part. You will steadily turn northwest and away from the road, climbing slightly. Watch the potholes.

1.7 *Cross over a tiny wetland. The stream washes over the road's surface during wet periods, but it's shallow.*

2.5 *On your right, just before you reach a rock barrier and a small house on the left (you're on Old Wawbeek Road), an unmarked trail heads into the woods. Take it.*

The first few feet of roots and rocky incline that you see from the road don't reflect the trail's true character, which improves quickly as you climb. You're in a magnificent spruce forest, practicing basic technical moves around rocks and roots and powering up across pine needle–covered singletrack flats. Very nice. Even fairly green intermediates won't have too much of a problem here, but it is moderately challenging (you can always walk). There are cross-country ski markers on the trees but none at the trailhead.

2.9 *Arrive at a Y, which to date remains unmarked. Take the left fork, which goes straight downhill.*

It continues to amaze me that the state leaves so much marking unattended and unmaintained, and this trail is a particular case in point. The cross-country ski trail, which went off to the right at the Y, rejoins the main trail shortly.

3.1 *Cross a little wetland bridge.*

3.4 *At the end of a descent, you'll see Mosquito Pond on your left.*

They don't call it that for nothing. You can't dawdle here, and there's no place convenient to sit near the pond. Go along the water's edge, pushing your bike past a few rocky spots, and remount to enjoy the trail's previous ridability.

4.4 *Following another descent, arrive at Deer Pond.*

Don't worry, you don't have to regain all of this elevation—you've already paid for it on the way in. An unmarked and insignificant spur trail appears to your left; it goes a short distance to a boat launch, where there are two old aluminum rowboats. Judging by the duct tape covering their hulls, I don't advise punting. Just before crossing a bridge back on the main trail, a pretty beaver pond is off to the right, and an "established" spot flat enough for a tent is next to it. It's actually illegal to camp within 150 feet of water or trails, except in established sites. But what determines whether or not a site is "established?" The interpretation depends on the local forest ranger.

Cross the bridge and continue.

4.6 *Arrive at a Y where at this writing there are two state trail signs lying on the ground, each leaning against large maple trees.*

The Gangway—Watch that middle groove!

Assuming nobody played any tricks, one sign indicates that you've come 3 miles from the NY 30 parking area, which is considerably in error (to avoid frustration, confusion, and disorientation, never try to make sense out of state trail signs). To the left, the trail is not marked, but this little side trip (the trail itself continues for several privately owned miles to Lead Pond) is the best part of the tour.

Follow downhill a few hundred feet, until you reach a point close to the lake's edge.

Look around to your left a bit, and you'll discover a large rock overlooking the pond. This area has been royally trashed by thoughtless campers, and I found a big garbage bag full of beer and soda cans here. The soil is heavily impacted by fires and encampments (in other words, it's "established"). Tread lightly—this is a special place. This is also the best place to rest and eat or swim, and the water in Deer Pond is very clear and and inviting. The trail continues along, toward Lead Pond. I followed it only a short distance before turning around, but it did appear that there's a small beach at Deer Pond's north end. I also made inquiries as to the status of the cut-off trail through Deer Pond Marsh to Whey Pond since it would make a logical road connection back to NY 30 through Rollins and Fish Creek Pond Public Campground. "How is that trail?" I later asked a local woodsman. "Underwater," was all he said.

Go back up to the intersection at 4.6 miles, and bear left to continue on the loop, heading toward Bull Point (not your destination) and the NY 30 parking area.

Follow a nice little singletrack of compacted soil along the edge of a hill through a second-growth forest of deciduous trees. Descend to a point where you cross a few plank bridges and the going gets a little soggy. I found a bike tire and a tube decorating a tree at this point (thanks a lot).

5.8 *Cross a plank bridge above a narrow creek within a small wetland that feeds the Raquette River.*

The bridge is starting to rot, so watch it. The trail is skinny and fast here.

6.1 *Get up onto a very long, double-planked gangway now, and follow it for about 1,000 feet, resisting the temptation to ride it.*

Hotshots *will* want to ride it—but it's a good way to bend a rim or break your jaw. This otherworldly thoroughfare passes through a moist realm of balsam fir and fiddleheads, the kind of dark, mythic forest from which folk and fairytales spring, and lands on an easy, spaghetti-thin singletrack with little or no obstacles.

6.4 *Reach a Y with—remarkably!—an intact trail sign. Turn right for the remaining 1.2-mile ride back to the parking area.*
Bull Point is out to your left at 0.7 mile. There's no actual point, just a road ride back to your car if you go this way. Yours is a wide, doubletrack treadway through a forest of mixed evergreens and maturing white pines. It's flat and fast, without obstacles. Watch for walkers.

7.7 *At a T, bear left (sorry, no sign). There's a trashy primitive campsite here.*

7.8 *Hit the tar road you came in on, and go left (again, no sign).*

7.85 *Go through the barrier gate, and arrive at your car.*
This trail has received a lot of attention in shop handouts, county guides, and maps, and in a trail book or two about skiing and hiking. On my way out to Dumas', I stopped in at World Cup (the bike shop in Tupper), and recognized the Spinergys. There I met Mr. Sabin, the local off-road guru. Stop in and say hello, and drool a bit over Mike's downhill hardware. He's got maps and info.

Camping Permits and General Information

Forest Ranger Headquarters: NYSDEC, Route 86, Box 296, Ray Brook, NY 12977-0296: 518-897-1200

Bike Shops:

Barkeater Bike Shop, 49 Main Street, Saranac Lake, NY: 518-891-5207; 1-800-254-5207

World Cup Ski, Board, and Bike, 68 Park Street, Tupper Lake, NY: 518-359-9481; e-mail: worldcup@tvenet.com

13
The St. Regis River Ride

Location: *Franklin County, Towns of Waverly, Santa Clara; St. Regis Canoe Area, Debar Mt. Wild Forest; Resource Management classified private lands*

Distance: *50 miles round-trip*

Surface Conditions: *Hard-packed dirt and sand roads*

Difficulty: *Suitable for all abilities, depending on the section and mileage chosen*

Maps: *Adirondack Canoe Map (does not contain entire route); USGS: St. Regis Mountain, Meno, Santa Clara, Meacham Lake (highly recommended for this tour); it is advisable to supplement the above with a quality Franklin County road map*

Highlights: *Long dirt road touring in remote atmosphere; proximity to St. Regis Canoe Area, Adirondack Visitor's Interpretive Center, primitive campsites, and Meacham Lake State Campground*

This is a long tour, suited to only those well prepared for a challenging, distance outing, that provides no available services or public buildings en route. Similar to the Black Fly Challenge in distance and difficulty (although flatter), cyclists will encounter even fewer cars and people on this backcountry ride. What you will encounter is a serenity unusual to most of the bike rides you've taken, and you'll get a look at a large swath of the Adirondack Park that not too many people use or even realize exists. Suggestions within the text will give you some ideas for shortening the distance and shuttling.

One of the most spectacular areas of the entire park is accessible near the beginning of this tour in Paul Smiths—at the St. Regis Canoe Area, a series of ponds connected by short portage trails where no motorboats are permitted. (This area is also referred to by its older, more romanti-

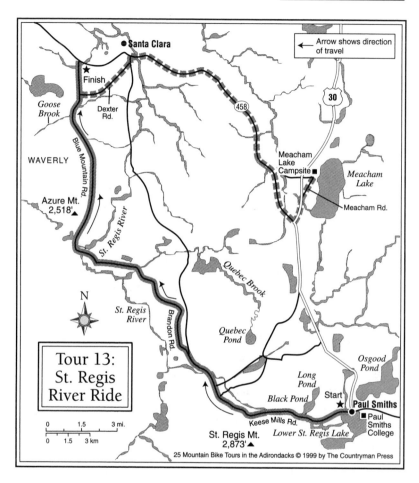

Santa Clara

Arrow shows direction
of travel

Finish

Goose
Brook

Dexter
Rd.

458

30

WAVERLY

Blue Mountain Rd.

Meacham
Lake
Campsite ■

Meacham
Lake

Azure Mt.
2,518'▲

Meacham Rd.

St. Regis River

N

Quebec Brook

St. Regis
River

Brandon Rd.

Quebec
Pond

Osgood
Pond

**Tour 13:
St. Regis
River Ride**

Long
Pond

Black Pond

Start
★

Paul Smiths

Paul
Smiths
College

| 0 | 1.5 | 3 mi. |
| 0 | 1.5 | 3 km |

Keese Mills Rd.

St. Regis Mt.
2,873'▲

Lower St. Regis Lake

25 Mountain Bike Tours in the Adirondacks © 1999 by The Countryman Press

cally appealing name, the Route of the Seven Carries.) It is the only such single-use designation in the park. If you have the inclination to travel with a canoe on your roof, don't miss an overnight or two in this remarkable place. Details and logistics can be worked out using the Adirondack Canoe Routes map or any number of Adirondack (north flow) canoe-route books and publications. But you can also stop "on the fly" at Paul Smiths College when school is in session and ask for information at the college store. Purchase a St. Regis area topographic map, which is all you'll need for navigational purposes and for locating portage trails. Adirondack Maps Inc.'s Adirondack Canoe Map is, however, the best map in existence for using the St. Regis Canoe Area. There's a public easement and canoe launch on the college campus itself.

Local paddlers and visiting regulars will tell you that there is simply no place like the St. Regis. These are not the busy ponds and lakes of Fish Creek, the Fulton Chain, or the Saranacs—where high-speed boaters pulling skiers and parasailers crowd the waterways—but a magically peaceful, loon-populated sanctuary that is well encamped during the late-summer tourist season with a kindred fraternity of canoeists. The key to enjoying the area is to "go light." You can camp in lean-tos or on the water's edge in "established" campsites (previously impacted ground that the Department of Environmental Conservation recognizes as legal, even though they may be closer than the required 150-foot distance from trails or water sources).

Other opportunities for free primitive camping abound in this part of the park. The St. Regis River itself, from Lower St. Regis Lake all the way down to the Black Pond–Long Ponds Recreation Area on Keese Mills Road, has several lean-tos, and tent camping is also legal. There are several lean-tos within a ten-minute paddle of either Paul Smiths College or the Black Pond parking lot on the St. Regis River. Both Black and Long Ponds (five lean-tos), and several of the surrounding ponds, are special brook trout water, each with shelters within a 20-minute paddle. Other ponds and lakes in the area also have lean-tos and are worth checking out. Look at your map, and note the shelters and campsites on Osgood, Jones, and Mountain Ponds as well as along the Blue Dot Reservoir Trail. Some you can drive to. Each has attractive tent sites. Most can be reached on foot. Along the tour route, opportunities for camping on state forest-preserve lands exist. Come prepared to enjoy your off time! This is the ideal place to shake down for that distance tour you've always wanted to do—the one where you can go light, carry a small tent, a summer-weight sleeping bag, a good book, and maybe a fishing rod. As usual, carry plenty of water, and don't drink any untreated water.

Begin at the intersection of NY 30 and NY 28, right across the street from Paul Smiths College, in a large dirt parking area with a lean-to. Just across NY 30 from this lot is Keese Mills Road, where you begin. Alternate plans and shuttling arrangements should be considered at this point. Since this is a long day ride, you can shorten the trip at both ends according to your time constraints. One way to do this is to begin the tour at the Black Pond–Long Pond Recreation Area and fishing access parking lot, which you'll find 2.4 miles down Keese Mill Road. You can also start a few miles farther down, where several parking spaces exist along the road. Something to consider carefully is the possibility of being dropped off here at Keese Mills Road and having someone retrieve you up at the north end—where the tour ends on NY 458 near St. Regis Falls. A public campground is 15 miles southeast of there, at Meacham Lake on NY 30. And you can make an overnight of it, looping back to your car either on NY 30 (not a great biking road, even though it was the training route for the 1980 US Olympic Bicycling Team) or the way you came. The Adirondack Visitor's Interpretive Center is just up NY 30 at 0.7 mile. Take a spin through the college campus, and have a look at Lower St. Regis Lake and St. Regis Mountain (elevation 2,873').

0.0 *Head down Keese Mills Road. This section is paved. Pass by houses and camps.*

2.4 *Across from the St. Regis Presbyterian Church (the prettiest church in five counties), you'll see the Black Pond–Long Pond parking area.*

On the other side of the road is the extreme north end of Lower St. Regis Lake, the headwaters of the St. Regis River. To the right is a dam and the beginning of the free-flowing river (until it's dammed again in St. Regis Falls). The road is still paved, has no shoulders, and very little traffic. The topography is gently rolling, with some views of the river amid open woodlands.

3.5 *Here is a large pull-off where you could park, just at the Santa Clara town line.*

4.4 *Cross the St. Regis River.*

Enjoy mountain views and tall white pines here.

4.9 *Pass a small parking space.*

5.8 *Enter a black spruce forest.*

6.3 *Pass the caretaker's cottage at Bay Pond (this land belongs to the Rockefellers), and bear right.*

Pass through burned-over lands—the site of a turn-of-the-century forest fire. You can still see stumps of large white pines that were destroyed. Pioneer species have sprung up everywhere, yet the scorched soil has not yet yielded a dominant forest type. The plain has an unusual alpine meadow quality. The Franklin County Adirondack Mountain Bike Trails Map—one of the best county-mountain-bike publications I've ever seen—calls this area a "blueberry barrens," and that about sums it up. Just be careful whose blueberries you pick; private-land sentiment tends to run high around here.

Now you're on Blue Mountain Road (also called Brandon Road, depending on which direction you're traveling); follow it all the way to NY 458 (if you want to).

7.2 Cross the river again.

7.3 Pass the first of several private roads on your right. A pine plantation with fern undergrowth follows, yielding views over the river on your left.

8.0 You are greeted with a seasonal-highway sign.

At this point you pass through a remote forest of scattered poplar, tall pines, and incongruous, posted right-of-ways. According to the county route description, here can be found the gray jay (normally associated with Canadian boreal forests) and the three-toed woodpecker—rare even in its preferred coniferous forest. These are black-backed birds whose male has a yellow crown. The cry is a sharp *pik*.

Here the surface is dirt, hard-packed sand, and loose gravel, having more the character of a trail than a road as you proceed. Some bogging down in sand can be anticipated. This inconvenience can be alleviated somewhat by letting a little air out of your tires—but don't do it unless you have a pump, and since letting too much air out can increase the possibilities of a flat, have tire tools, as well. Sand depth and consistency will depend a bit on moisture, season, and road maintenance (sand roads are best negotiated in colder weather).

10.2 A red pine plantation and boggy meadows appear.

11.7 Pass the gate to Camp Madawaska.

13.8 Cross Quebec Brook.

14.1 Views of Azure Mountain are on your right. Enter the township of Waverly. (No services.)

14.8 *Climb a significant hill.*

16.4 *Cross the river again, over a large bridge in the neighborhood of several cabins and small shanties.*

16.6 *Turn right at a T, and continue. More camps appear.*

17.5 *On your left is the Azure Mountain trailhead parking area.*

This large lot has a privy, and the short (0.75-mile) trail for the summit departs in a maturing spruce forest.

18.7 *Open scrub and uphill follow over the next few miles of dusty road.*

The surface washboards in spots, more and more camps appear, then residences. This is a good spot to turn around if you're not planning a through trip. Beyond, the road is anticlimactic.

22.4 *Hit pavement.*

22.9 *Cross Goose Pond Brook.*

Pass Browntrack Road on your left and Dexter Road on your right. (Dexter Road is the way to go if you're planning on riding to Meacham Lake Public Campground along NY 458. By doing so you'll cut off a particularly unattractive section of highway.)

23.3 *Top out on a hill.*

24.6 *Pass Santa Clara Road on your right.*

24.7 *Arrive at NY 458.*

About 3 miles to your right (east) is an excellent meeting place for anyone who is going to pick you up to wait. (Judging your arrival time will be difficult, especially if you have problems. Consider going the distance to the Meacham Lake Public Campground.) It's called the Santa Clara Flow Fishing Area Access Site and can be found on the south side of NY 458, 10 miles west of NY 30, which is convenient to the campground at Meacham Lake. But the shoulders are good here for most of the way, as is the scenery, and after slogging along on the loose surface of sandy dirt roads you've just left behind, you may just want a relatively fast ride back to the campsite. After all, what's another 15 miles? To reach the campsite from NY 458, just turn left on NY 30, and go another 2.5 miles north. This distance will be more pleasant if you turn right onto

Meacham Road just about 0.5 mile north of NY 458, instead of staying on NY 30, following the gauging station and bridge over Meacham Lake outlet (which forms the East Branch of the St. Regis River). This wooded road takes you to the central camping area. That will total your distance at roughly 40 miles, one way. Not a bad price to pay for such a memorable ride.

Camping Permits and General Information

Forest Ranger Headquarters: NYSDEC, Route 86, Box 296, Ray Brook, NY 12977-0296: 518-897-1200

Bike Shops

Barkeater Bike Shop, 49 Main Street, Saranac Lake, NY: 518-891-5207; 1-800-254-5207

World Cup Ski, Board, and Bike, 68 Park Street, Tupper Lake, NY: 518-359-9481; e-mail: worldcup@tvenet.com

14

The Dumas-Massawepie Sahara

Location: *St. Lawrence County, Town of Piercefield, Horseshoe Lake Wild Forest, private easement areas, Hancock Timber Resource Group*
Terrain: *Hilly and remote, densely forested*
Distance: *28 miles*
Surface Conditions: *Hard sand roads (loose, deep sand in a few places)*
Rating: *Advanced*
Maps: *The Adirondacks: Northwest Lakes; USGS: Piercefield*
Highlights: *Distance/endurance ride, scenery, isolation, exploration*
Restrictions: *No cycling on Massawepie Scout Reservation Lands June through August and "as posted" during specific timber harvesting periods in timber resource lands, with public access until the year 2004.*

Here's one you'll never forget because the effort to forget it will keep reminding you. Done in its entirety, this is strictly a tour for ironpersons, those Camelback and Lycra-laden, gelpak-sucking insect look-a-likes with their muticolored jerseys and wind goggles and bulging quads and $3,000 bikes who change into supermen and -women at the trailhead (they really *can* fly). This is not a tour for wimps or wannabes, and it's really not for groups like small families, who as a rule tend to have a wide range of abilities coupled with low thresholds for abuse, torture, and dehydration. But if on the outside chance you do see an actual family pounding this lunar terrain, wearing ringlets of fine dust around their cheeks and sporting mud-stuccoed thighs as they blow only wet air through their water bottles, it won't be the Brady Bunch.

Prepare for an outing of 30-plus miles if you're looking to see Mr. Dumas, whose establishment lies on the outer fringe of the Childwold barrens just northwest of the Massawepie Reservation along NY 3.

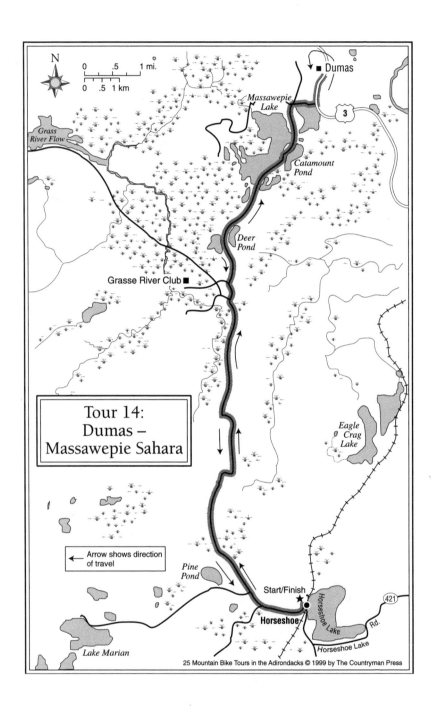

N

0   .5   1 mi.

0   .5   1 km

→ ■ Dumas

Massawepie Lake

3

Grass River Flow

Catamount Pond

Deer Pond

Grasse River Club ■

**Tour 14:
Dumas –
Massawepie Sahara**

Eagle Crag Lake

← Arrow shows direction
of travel

Pine Pond

Start/Finish ★

Horseshoe

Horseshoe Lake

421

Horseshoe Lake Rd.

Lake Marian

25 Mountain Bike Tours in the Adirondacks © 1999 by The Countryman Press

Dumas' has long been a watering hole for snowmobilers and the staff members at Massawepie scout camp (those boys don't drink just bug juice, you know), and his establishment makes for a logical halfway destination as you pass through the void and find yourself in need of a high-volume caloric jolt and something to swig it down with. Prepare for an outing of closer to 50 miles if you "plan" to return to Horseshoe by road, as I did. And plan even more carefully if you intend to poke your nose around in the boggy upcountry of Burntbridge Outlet and Grass River Flow, which is also open to all-terrain bikers.

Should you make the decision to "cross the void"—which in reality is a fine yet demanding cross-country-ride experience, though you can always turn around—first get yourself to Horseshoe Lake. Find Horseshoe Lake Road (CR 421) by traveling south from Tupper Lake about 10 miles. It's well identified. Turn right (west) here, and go nearly 7 miles, heading straight all the way to the end of the road, where you'll find primitive campsites next to the lake (there are a bunch of attractive primitive sites and picnic areas just as you get on this road, too, around the Bog River Picnic Area). This is Horseshoe, an old station stop of Augustus Low's Horseshoe Forestry Company Railway, which dates from 1893. This station was still in service in 1965. This is a nice camping spot, if not a bit isolated for the timid folks among us. But, hey, if you were timid, you wouldn't be here now. And you wouldn't use the smelly latrines that are across the tracks and straight back on the left.

You'll see the railroad tracks right behind you—assuming you're looking out at the lake—first. Make sure you have much water, your bike tools, patches, a pump, sunscreen, insect repellent, maps, a large food or energy-bar supply, and all that. Hop on your mountain bike (hybrid junkies will suffer), and set to zero.

0.0 Cross the tracks and head directly to your left, following the wide sandy road that will be your friend for a while.

You'll see little handmade Dumas signs on your left, indicating the distance to that oasis at 14 miles. You will be decorously escorted by squadrons of brilliant, curious dragonflies if you're lucky (they eat blackflies). You may see little scrums of yellow swallowtail butterflies huddled in the road—and by the looks of their scattered wing parts, lying like sad, yellow strips of filigree along the sand—

they do not lift off adroitly. Please give way! You're a guest here. Happy so far?

0.9 Encounter a STOP barrier at a Y. The left goes to Hitchins. You go right.

1.3 At this Y, bear right. The left goes to Otter Brook, a private club.

1.4 Go around a barrier.

2.0 At this intersection, bear left, following along the northeast edge of Pine Pond.

2.6 Reach another barrier.

2.7 Arrive in a large sand pit. Keep bearing right, and you will find yourself on another wide sand road.

Keep alert and watch to the right.

2.75 See the DUMAS sign on your right? No? Then somebody ripped it down. Bear right here through a barrier with two stop signs on it.

This is the snowmobile trail to Dumas'. It's a jeep road, with two distinct ruts and a grassy strip in the middle. You can cruise to 15 mph here, and it's a nice change from the sand. Don't bank on seeing anyone else too soon, but stay alert. Signs of 4x4s are everywhere. (These roads are in excellent shape. After 8 miles, I punched up an average of 9.1 mph.)

3.4 In a hardwood forest, you hit a Y. A barrier is to the right. Go left. There are some old snowmobile markers around.

3.6 Perhaps you'll see the small pond down to the right.

3.75 Intersect with a wide sand road, the same one you got off to get on the Dumas road back at mile 2.75.

You'll see conservation easement signs now, telling you that this is a private forest management and public recreation area, courtesy of the Hancock Timber Resource Group in concert with the NYS Department of Environmental Conservation. Thanks all around. Get up on the sand road and bear right. Those little orange markers with the white diamonds are universal snowmobile indicators.

Crossing the void

4.3 At a T, the intersection with another wide sand road that comes in from parts unknown to your right, bear left at the friendly Dumas sign.

By now you're expecting the Taj Mahal, right? Go through a red pine plantation (you'll be reading newsprint from these someday), then a Scotch pine plantation, where someone hung up an old, ugly neon sign saying LIQUOR STORE. See if it's still there (this is snowmobile humor).

5.1 A wide sandy road goes off to the right. We go straight.

Deer tracks are everywhere. More roads intersect, but I won't bother to spell them all out. Just continue straight on the main drag. It's obvious because most intersecting roads come in at right angles.

5.8 Pass a hunting camp on your right that looks like a nice private residence.

5.9 Go through a barrier.

7.8 Arrive at a major road junction, called Junction 2, a.k.a. "no man's land and then some." We will go straight here.

Signs to the left indicate NY 3, Cranberry Lake, and South Colton (out to NY 3 at Shurtleff along Grass River Flow). You could form a large loop by taking this left, going west-northwest out to NY 3 and coming back south through Massawepie—if you're feeling hardcore. To the right are signs to Conifer, a little village with no stores, across the Emporium Easement, but this crosses private land (though it's the quickest bail-out point in an emergency to NY 3 and Tupper Lake).

Go straight toward Massawepie.

As I fussed with my maps and slaked my thirst here, a lone raven grokked a solitary hello and flapped lazily in the direction of Dead Creek. I started whistling theme songs from spaghetti Westerns when I sensed encroaching delirium. Time for a raspberry energy bar.

There are a couple more noteworthy signs here. One says CAUTION, XC SKIERS ON TRAIL (you know those dangerous types), and a sign pointing back insists it's 9.3 miles to Horseshoe Lake. They must have taken a different route, I guess. Hey—no signs for Dumas'! (It's straight ahead.) Onward!

8.2 Pass a road with signs to the Grass River Club on the left. Enter Otetiana Council, Boy Scouts of America property.

Keep tooling along on this wide sand road. You're at elevation 1,685'.

9.1 Things start to get pretty now, and you feel like you're coming out of the desert into the oasis transition zone.

Deer Pond is down to the right.

10.5 *Now it's very pretty, sort of an alpine lakes environment.*

Massawepie Lake opens up on your left as you drift downhill amid a hemlock wood in an ideal Adirondack setting.

Pedal past the scout reservation's outbuildings, fields, and lodges until finally passing the ranger headquarters.

13.0 *Arriving at NY 3, turn left for Dumas'.*

14.0 *Arrive and imbibe.*

Should you wish to turn around now, going home the way you came, by all means, it's the fastest way back. If you choose to go by road, you're looking at about a 35-miler back up into Horseshoe Lake. Shoulders vary on NY 3 but are generally good, though traffic tends to be fast in my experience. Because I was riding on slick tires, I had a pleasant journey of it, but I don't advise it. After all, it's only 13 dirt miles back from Massawepie, and you did want to explore some more, didn't you?

On the way back into Horseshoe, I ran into Julie, a road biker who was finishing out a century ride when her rear tire blew. She was swarmed by blackflies and had no repellent, so I loaned her mine. I wasn't much help fixing the tube, but I'm adept at drawing flies.

Camping Permits and General Information

Forest Ranger Headquarters: NYSDEC, 6739 U.S. Highway 11, Potsdam, NY 13676: 315-265-3090

Bike Shops

Barkeater Bike Shop, 49 Main Street, Saranac Lake, NY: 518-891-5207; 1-800-254-5207

World Cup Ski, Board, and Bike, 68 Park Street, Tupper Lake, NY: 518-359-9481; e-mail: worldcup@tvenet.com

15

William C. Whitney Area and Lake Lila

Location: *Hamilton County, Town of Long Lake, Lake Lila Primitive Area*
Distance: *16.6 miles, plus 7.4 miles of alternate route*
Terrain: *Gently rolling*
Surface Conditions: *Dirt and gravel roads, minor sections of
    pavement*
Rating: *Intermediate*
Maps: *The Adirondacks: Northwest Lakes; USGS: Little Tupper Lake*
Highlights: *William C. Whitney Area canoe and hiking access trails;
    access to long, scenic gravel roads; swimming at Lake Lila*

At this time there is a "no mountain bikes" policy at the William C.
Whitney Area, the newest large acquisition to the New York State Forest
Preserve near Tupper Lake. While as of this writing the area has not yet
been classified as either wilderness or wild forest, it is being managed as
a wilderness. The interim management plan now in effect waits for the
official classification of these lands by the Adirondack Park Agency, the
park's land-use planning and regulatory agency. At that point, public
hearings will be held, and public participation will be encouraged. Some
environmental groups and countless individuals are interested in seeing
this area classified as wilderness. In particular, the Adirondack Council,
which has done more for the preservation of the Adirondacks than any
other nonprofit organization, has lobbied for and would like to see all of
these holdings, along with the Five Ponds Wilderness Area, combined
into a new entity called the Bob Marshall Wilderness Area.

At this time, the state land-use master plan allows for individual use
designations for bicycles in wild forest, primitive, and canoe areas. NYS
Lands and Forests officials have not ruled out the possibility that at least
part of this holding will become a canoe area, in which case Burn Road

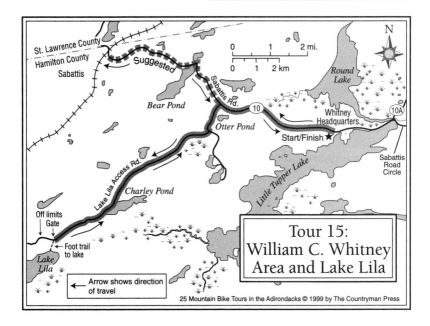

Tour 15:
William C. Whitney
Area and Lake Lila

25 Mountain Bike Tours in the Adirondacks © 1999 by The Countryman Press

and others may ultimately be opened to bikes. Because of the Whitney's flat, extensive road system, it's not unreasonable to expect that these may be made legal in the future, especially if the appropriate classifications are made.

The 15,000-acre acquisition, representing a large holding within the Whitney estate, was rescued from land development, which proposed to build half-million dollar houses along the shores of Little Tupper Lake, the area's principal body of water. Now that the state has paid $17 million for the transfer, the land is yours and mine. This tour will take you past the Whitney area, and to its headquarters, on a scenic road to Lake Lila. Lake Lila is a worthy destination, but the road to it is bumpy and long. This is an ideal place to split your party between those who want to bike and those who would prefer to canoe in Little Tupper Lake. You can launch at the headquarters' parking area. The lake has designated campsites, and at this time it is very popular with canoeists.

To gain access to the area from Tupper Lake, head south 11 miles on NY 30 to Sabattis Road (also referred to as Sabattis Circle Road and CR 10A). Turn right, follow for 3.1 miles to a Y, and bear right, going another mile to the headquarters' road on your left. From Long Lake, go north on NY 30 for 7 miles. Turn left onto Sabattis Road (a.k.a. Sabattis Circle Road and CR 10A). At 2.4 miles you'll pass the Stony Pond Trailhead on your left (no bikes—at this time the trail is a wheelchair-accessible horse and foot trail). At 2.9 miles, you'll reach a Y. Turn left here and go another mile to the headquarters' road on your left.

Follow the headquarters' road past an information booth and a pair of latrines, and go down to the parking lot at the water's edge. You should be able to get a map of the area at the information booth. Get your bike ready, and head back out of the headquarters, setting to zero and resuming your ride along Sabattis Road. Because parking is not permitted along this road, it's best to begin from the headquarters' parking lot, where your vehicle will be secure. It's 3.2 easy miles to the Lake Lila access road.

0.0 *Turn left onto (paved) Sabattis Road.*

1.5 *Pass an access road on your left.*

3.2 *Turn left onto the Lake Lila access road, where a rocky and hilly dirt road will take you to the Lake Lila parking area.*

3.3 *Pass Otter Pond on your left.*

3.7 *Pass a private road on your left. Soon you begin to climb.*

7.1 *Pass Charley Pond on your left.*

7.4 *A private house appears on your right.*

8.1 *Pass a gated road on your left.*

8.3 *A wetland on your right forms the soggy backwater of Lake Lila's ancient perimeter.*

Arrive immediately at the parking area where you'll see a sign-board showing the destinations to Lake Lila via the service road, which is in front of you on the right and closed to bikes. The Nehasane Lodge site, the former home of the Webb family, is at 3.2 miles, and Mt. Frederick (elevation 2,200') is 4.5 miles. Because of its location in the Lake Lila Primitive Area, this road is off-limits to bikes, but it's frequently traveled by service vehicles. It's not legal to walk or ride your bike the 0.3 mile down to the lake on the canoe access path you'll see heading south from the parking lot. Lock up your bike at the trailhead and walk down to the sand beach and expansive views of the lake you'll get on this short trail. Watch out for portaging canoeists—they can't see you well from under their boats.

If you're in the mood for more distance, or if you want to skip the Lake Lila road altogether, the gravel road out to Sabattis also makes a good and much easier ride. It continues another 3.7 miles beyond the Lake Lila access road, passing several ponds and wetlands until ending at the private lands of the Robinwood Club and Sabattis-Hiawatha Scout Reservation. Sabattis Station, which stood next to the Remsen–Lake Placid Travel Corridor, once stood at this point.

Retrace your route back to the headquarters and your car.

Camping Permits and General Information

Forest Ranger Headquarters: NYSDEC, 6739 U.S. Highway 11, Potsdam, NY 13676: 315-265-3090

Bike Shops

Barkeater Bike Shop, 49 Main Street, Saranac Lake, NY: 518-891-5207; 1-800-254-5207

World Cup Ski, Board, and Bike, 68 Park Street, Tupper Lake, NY: 518-359-9481; e-mail: worldcup@tvenet.com

III. LAKE GEORGE REGION

16

Pack Demonstration Forest

Location: *Warren County, Town of Warrensburg*
Terrain: *Flat, with one long climb*
Distance: *Forest loop, 6.2 miles; Plantation loop, 4.4 miles*
Surface conditions: *Well-drained dirt and sand roads*
Rating: *Beginner*
Maps: *The Adirondacks: Lake George Region; USGS: The Glen; Pack Forest Trail Map (handout when available); 1941 Pack Compartment Map (by request)*
Highlights: *Proximity to Lake George Campgrounds; a lake supporting a good bass fishery; canoes permitted; hiking and nature trails; views of the southeastern Adirondacks; State University of New York College of Environmental Science and Forestry instruction field base; marked and maintained trails; on-site caretaker*

Unexpectedly rustic yet accessible, with open, easy dirt-road riding through highly managed forests, the 2,700-acre Pack Demonstration Forest is an ideal day trip from the Lake George area. Surrounded by wetlands and scenic low hills, this controlled forest gives you the feel of a much larger and "forever wild" wilderness environment. Located roughly 4.5 miles north of the confluence (near Thurman Station) of the Schroon River to the east, and the Hudson (a short ride away) to the west, the terrain is gently rolling, and the one "strenuous" climb to the low summit of Ben Wood Mountain, with its excellent view of the southeastern Adirondacks, can be avoided by you flat footers if necessary. There are no big rocks or difficult obstacles in the trails, and there's no singletrack. It's all an easy ride with a comfortable, secure feel to it.

The Charles Lathrop Pack Demonstration Forest is a regional cam-

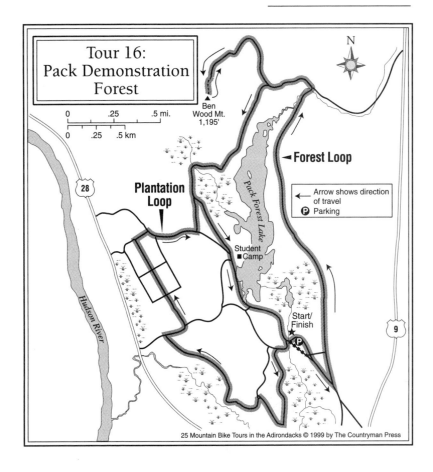

Tour 16:
Pack Demonstration
Forest

N

Ben
Wood Mt.
1,195'

0   .25   .5 mi.

0   .25   .5 km

◄ **Forest Loop**

**Plantation
Loop** ▼

Pack Forest Lake

Arrow shows direction
of travel
Ⓟ Parking

28

Student
■ Camp

Hudson River

Start/
Finish
★
Ⓟ

9

25 Mountain Bike Tours in the Adirondacks © 1999 by The Countryman Press

pus belonging to the State University of New York's College of Environmental Science and Forestry (ESF). There are several such campuses in the park, each contributing to ESF's education, research, and demonstration programs. Among these, near Cranberry Lake, is Wanakena, one of the most noted forest ranger schools in the country. The Newcomb Campus (Huntington Forest), located 10 miles east of Long Lake, is now the site of an Adirondack Visitor Center, which you are strongly encouraged to visit.

ESF programs include the nine general areas of chemistry, environmental and forest biology, environmental studies, forest engineering, forest technology, landscape architecture, paper science and engineering, resource management, and wood products engineering. Knowing this makes a trip to Pack Forest not only a great outing to a skillfully manipulated natural environment, but an educational experience as well. You'll be fascinated by the extensive white pine plantations and wetlands that serve the college's research efforts. In addition, the Forest also features hiking and interpretive foot trails, and permits fishing and hunting in-season. It is closed to all-terrain vehicles.

Pack Forest is situated off of NY 9 just north of the intersection with NY 28 in Warren County, about 10 miles north of Lake George, or just under 4 miles north of Warrensburg. Turn left off NY 9 at the sign for Pack Demonstration Forest, and go 0.6 mile to the parking area. A small office is located here, plus a registry with (maybe) a map posted inside it. Obtaining maps can be a problem, since the office isn't staffed around the clock, but you will be able to navigate from the map in this book. Unfortunately, it doesn't contain the kind of useful detail that a plantation zone like Pack Forest requires. Barring any more recent offerings, these highlights can be found on the very precise and beautifully drawn March 1941 Compartment Map (compiled with student transit surveys and aerial photographs in 1938 and '39), and if you're lucky enough to arrive when the office is open (scheduling hours vary), the manager might give you one. At 3,000 acres, it's possible but not altogether scary or objectionable to "get lost" on the winding forest roads, and it can be equally dumbfounding and harmless to cruise amid the baffling gridwork of the inner plantation area. In a vigorous few hours of sumptuous riding, which will inevitably include a couple of dead-enders, it is possible to figure the whole place out. Or you can try to stick to the map.

Forest Loop

0.0 *Push off, pedaling back out the road you drove in on.*

0.03 *Turn left onto broken pavement.*

  You are riding on Old Route 9. Cruise blissfully.

1.4 *Pass a public fishing access road to your left.*

1.7 *Pass another public fishing access road.*

This isn't a plantation zone but a mixed forest, including hemlock, cedar, and pine.

2.1   *Arrive at an intersection.*

The road to the left is gated, and signs say DO NOT BLOCK GATE and ROAD CLOSED. Turn left, go around the gate, and follow the dirt road. Cataract Brook disappears into a wetland off to your left.

2.38 *Turn right at a Y, and go uphill.*

The road climbs steadily, turning slowly to the east.

3.10 *A small rocky area appears, with a poor view to the southeast.*

This isn't the top! Keep going.

3.20 *Arrive at the summit of Ben Wood Mountain (elevation 1,195').*

The view is good to the east. You can't see Lake George (well, maybe a few little spots), but many low peaks on the east side of the lake, looking toward Fort Ann and Whitehall, can be surveyed. South to north, these include French Mountain (1,319'), Pilot Knob (2,165'), Buck Mountain (2,330'), probably Cat Mountain (1,955') west of the lake in the northerly foreground, and a proud collection of rag-tag lumps that stretch out into the rumpled blue-green hills of the Tongue Mountain Range . . . the veritable heart of the southern Adirondacks. There are so many, it's difficult to make a positive ID on any but the largest without triangulating with an orienteering compass—but who cares?

This is the suggested lunch spot, though the deerflies may refute me. Otherwise, there are very good places on the lake, as well (also with deerflies). There's no shortcut down the mountain, so return gingerly to the Y intersection back down the hill (mile 2.38).

4.09 *Turn right at the Y, and ride along a flat dirt road, with plot #54 (on the 1941 Compartment Map) to your right.*

4.5   *Views of the lake begin around here.*

4.6   *Pass a fishing access road on the left.*

You can explore these—they're all dead-ends. Continue, passing between a wetland and forest. Observe a beaver dam and beaver house beyond, each in the company of pickerel weed and lilies with a backdrop of low hills. Keep going.

5.00 *At a Y, continue on the "main drag" (still dirt), bearing left as more wetlands follow on your east (left).*

Arrive at a group of buildings (student camp) set along the lake in plot #50. Ben Wood Mountain seems to have vanished! It looms up behind you in the distance.

5.62 *Pass another public fishing access site.*

You might see canoeists around. Did you bring yours?

6.10 *Go through the gate by the caretaker's house, and turn left, going uphill toward the barn and sawmill and the public parking area where your car is.*

6.20 *Arrive at your car.*

Plantation Loop

You've seen the eastern half of Pack Demonstration Forest, a varied collection of forest types, in a mountain and wetland setting. Now you're headed into the plantation area, where you will witness various stages of forest succession in a highly controlled yet natural environment.

0.0 *Leave the parking lot, and turn right at the first road you come to (shortcut in front of the shed). Drop down onto the road, bear right, head northwest past the caretaker's cottage again (this time in the opposite direction from the Forest Loop), cross a creek and go through a gate, and bear left at the Y.*

0.32 *Go through another gate, keeping the creek to your left.*

Glide downhill a little.

0.43 *Bear left at a Y.*

0.60 *Pass the nature trail on your left.*

Take a moment to stop here. Leave your bikes, and walk up the trail about 150 feet to see the Grandmother Tree, an enormous and stately white pine the way they use to make them. It's on the right side of the trail just before the boardwalk; you can't miss it.

1.1 *At a Y, turn left (two quick lefts, in reality) into a white-pine plantation.*

1.25 *You pass through a red-pine plantation.*

1.30 *At a Y, bear right. (If you were to turn left here, you'd cross Millington Brook and hit the road to Warrensburg.)*

1.5 *Pass through a red-pine forest with a white-pine understory.*

1.93 *At a T, turn right into a highly ordered plantation of skinny red pine.*

2.03 *Turn left at a T, among maturing red pine.*

2.23 *Go straight, through a four-way intersection, leaving a small plot of Pinus banksiana (Jack pines) on your right.*

2.43 *At another Y intersection, go straight again.*

The ground is covered with reindeer moss in this area.

2.62 *At a T, go right.*

2.72 *At a Y, bear right.*

Within a very short distance you'll see two roads coming in from the right.

Take the left fork, going uphill (not the right, which is level).

Climb into a mixed, wild forest.

3.12 *At a Y, in a thick plantation plot, turn left, going gently downhill.*

3.22 *At a T, turn right. You're back on the "main drag."*

Follow this, passing the student dormitory area and the Ecology Study Site. Continue with the lake to your left.

4.20 *Arrive back at the gate by the caretaker's house. Go through the gate, and turn left, heading up toward the parking area.*

4.40 *You're back at your car.*

If you've got the time and want to take a close look at a very scenic stretch of the Hudson River, go south on NY 9, back to the intersection of with NY 28, and turn right. Go about 2 miles, and turn left onto CR 40. The Hudson will appear on your right. There is legal public access along this fine stretch of water and a few places to pull over. The Hudson is shallow in the summertime, and you can wade across it in spots. Continue south on CR 40 into Warrensburg.

Information

Director of Forest Properties, SUNY College of Environmental Science and Forestry, Syracuse, NY 13210: 315-470-6500

Bike Shops

Inside Edge Ski and Bike Shop, 624 Upper Glen Road (NY 9), Glens Falls, NY: 518-793-5676

The Bike Shop, 368 Ridge Road (corner of Ridge and and Quaker Roads), Glens Falls, NY: 518-793-8986

FlipFlop Cycle Shop, 175 Canada Street, Lake George, NY: 518-668-2233

17
Shelving Rock Bay

Location: Warren County, Town of Fort Ann, Lake George Wild Forest
Distance: 10 miles
Terrain: Extremely hilly
Surface Conditions: Old carriage roads, dirt roads, and trails
Rating: Advanced
Maps: The Adirondacks: Lake George Region; USGS: Shelving Rock;
   ADK: Trails of the Eastern Adirondack Region (best), Eastern Region
Highlights: Convenient to Lake George village; secluded swimming and
   picnicking spots; primitive camping; miles of unresearched, designated
   trails to explore

Located in the (very) hilly country of Lake George's southeast shore, this tour represents only a minute fraction of the tremendous off-road cycling opportunities present in the Lake George Wild Forest. Because there is a 1,000' elevation difference between the Upper Hogtown Parking Area, where this tour begins, and the shoreline of the lake, which is its highlight, it will be enjoyed mostly by expert riders possessing a high level of fitness and an interest in challenging hills. That's not to say that any rider who's interested in seeing this magnificent arena of lakeside and mountain scenery can't do so, since there are some dirt roads and flat trails that surround the area as well and since increased levels of fitness can only be attained through a certain amount of struggle (you can always walk). These trails can be seen on maps as well as by a limited car tour of the region, where it is even possible to drive very near the lake by descending Shelving Rock Road to stage a tour from one of the lower parking or camping areas—in themselves attractive destinations. It is even legal to drive through the Upper Hogtown Parking Area into Dacy Clearing on a dirt road, accessing the many primitive camping sites and

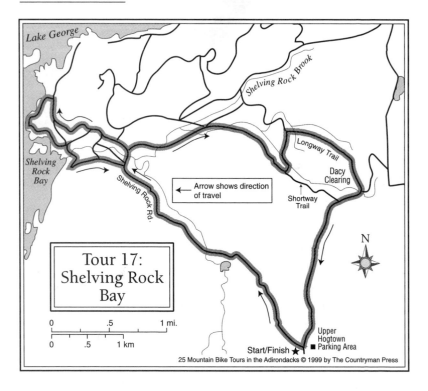

Lake George

Shelving Rock Brook

Longway Trail

Dacy Clearing

Arrow shows direction of travel

Shelving Rock Bay

Shortway Trail

Shelving Rock Rd.

N

Tour 17:
Shelving Rock
Bay

0   .5   1 mi.
0   .5   1 km

Upper
Hogtown
Parking Area

Start/Finish

25 Mountain Bike Tours in the Adirondacks © 1999 by The Countryman Press

bike-legal footpaths leading to the horse trails assembly area at the Sleeping Beauty trailhead.

To reach the area, get off the Adirondack Northway (I-87) at NY 149–Queensbury, Exit 20. Take a left off the northbound exit and, within 0.3 mile, your first right onto NY 149. Enter the Adirondack Park at 3.5 miles. Don't make the easy mistake at 5.2 miles of going left (north) onto NY 9L where a sign says LAKE GEORGE, EAST SHORE. Instead, keep going straight until at 6.6 miles you'll go left onto Buttermilk Falls Road, which bears left onto Sly Pond Road later on. At 11.6 miles, the road turns into dirt. At 17 miles, bear left onto Hogtown Road; you may see horse-trail markers on the trees. At 17.8 miles, pull into the Upper Hogtown Parking Area. Assemble your bike, air your tires, top out your water bottles, and don and strap your helmet. You're about to lose a thousand feet of elevation descending Shelving Rock Road. How are your brakes? Be careful here.

Partly owing to its extreme terrain, as well as to its relatively remote location, members of the biking community and its advocates have not developed maps or readily available information about this area. But anyone who takes a serious inventory of the resources here must feel that such developments are inevitable and exciting. Appreciable efforts can already be seen to have occurred on the state level. In the Generic Bicycle Amendment for Completed Adirondack Forest Preserve Unit Management Plans—in which the Black Mountain Section of the Lake George Wild Forest is described—it has been noted that the total distance of designated bicycle trails in the unit is now at a generous 38.4 miles. Forest management does not expect future high levels of use from bicyclists, however, and notes that the use levels of all user groups aren't notably evident at this time. Reassuringly (and this goes for the majority of Adirondack trails to date), according to the amendment, "No conflicts between bicyclists and other user groups have been reported to the local forest ranger." Trail surfaces are considered to be stable, particularly on the old carriage roads that exist in the area. Unstable surfaces, which occur mostly on trails that are remote and steep, will by nature of their terrain limit excessive use. Here we see effective management at work, employing the ideology that trails should be designed—or existing trails designated through individual evaluation—for the particular user group in mind. Such fledgling advances toward acceptance through the creation of established user patterns is cause for both gratitude and celebration within the cycling community. The age of the ATB, and its recognition as a means of legitimate recreational use, has arrived, which is something you couldn't have said just a few years back.

Naturally, as you ride, the quirky appearance of Murphy's Law—and the usual emergence of Peter's Principle (which submits that Murphy was an optimist)—will find you wondering if the same hand who designated some of these trails with a marking pen from an office chair belonged to the body of a downhill champ on steroids. Designated or not, this terrain is home to the die-hard enthusiast equipped with a bomb-proof outfit and a wicked sense of humor. Even as I rode along, I could see the guys in the forest management office, allotting each user group their respective slice of wild forest, hyperventilating with laughter, highlighters in hand, saying, "And here. We'll give *this* to the mountain bikers!"

0.0 *Leave the parking area, turn right, and descend steeply on the dirt Shelving Rock Road.*

Control your speed. If you're good with brakes, check those of your companions who are not. Trail signs abound, though none for your destination at the water's edge below.

0.5 *Pass trailheads to Dacy Clearing, Sleeping Beauty Mountain, and Fishbrook Ponds, some of which can be reached more easily on designated trails from where you parked.*

1.48 *Cross Shelving Rock Brook, and for a moment, climb.*

2.63 *Pass a camping area on your left.*

This is an attractive primitive area in a huge pine stand and the best place to camp if you're going to stay overnight.

2.65 *An unmarked horse trail and barrier gate appear on the right. Keep going straight.*

Pass another camping area, perhaps nicer than the first, and then a sign that says SPECIAL DAY USE AREA ONLY PAST THIS POINT.

2.94 *Pass another horse trail and small parking area on your right.*

3.24 *Pass another parking area.*

At the downhill end of it, a dirt road goes off into the woods. Keep going on the road for now, watching carefully on your left.

3.6 *Keep a lookout on your left for a tiny trail.*

A few hundred yards ahead, Shelving Rock Road road dead-ends at a private property sign. A few hundred feet downhill of the parking lot you just passed, watch carefully on your left for an unmarked trail that heads into the woods between two posts. You may have to search briefly for this trail.

0.0 *When you find it, set to zero again (it will be helpful later on), and follow along a fairly technical little stretch downhill toward the lake.*

0.2 *Once at the lake's edge, turn left and pass several small, secluded rocks that lie along the shore.*

These are popular picnicking destinations for those in the know. From these shelving rocks, you can see far up and down the lake to the Tongue Mountain Range in the north and east to the Hen and Chicken Islands, Crown and Green Islands, and Lake George's eastern shoreline and the mountains beyond. To the south across Shelving Rock Bay is Pilot Knob.

Continue along the carriage road—which has a character more like a wide trail at this point—keeping the lake on your right.

1.2 **Pass several more scenic spots, where you can explore on foot to the water's edge.**

You'll most likely see boats anchored here, each with a party of happy swimmers. The trail is well used, too, and many people claim the little romantic spots along peninsulas, sunning and diving into the incredibly clear waters between the mainland and Log Bay Island.

1.3 **At a Y, bear right.**

The left is the trail back to the parking lot discussed earlier (at the 3.2 mile mark).

1.5 **Cross a wooden bridge over Shelving Rock Brook.**

1.6 **Turn onto the trail on your left, which is the way out.**

You may elect to explore further along the old remnants of the carriageway, but my own efforts ended in blowdowns and rugged terrain within a few tenths of a mile. Climb up the trail, which is washed out in places but easily managed.

2.38 **Arrive at a dam and pond at the head of a small gorge carved by Shelving Rock Brook.**

2.4 **Turn left onto Shelving Rock Road and the bridge you passed earlier at mile 1.48. Turn left, and retrace your path briefly.**

2.5 **Pass the campsite area.**

2.58 **Turn right onto the unmarked horse trail, and easily go through the barrier gate.**

2.9 **Cross a wooden bridge, following the brook.**

Blue horse-trail markers and large yellow snowmobile markers show the way. The brook carves an attractive gorge on the left.

3.4 **Cross the brook.**

3.5 **Arrive at a T intersection, and go right.**

Signs here indicate Shelving Rock Road, Shelving Rock Mountain, and Dacy Clearing, the latter being your destination. Now climb steeply and steadily.

3.58 **Cross a plank bridge.**

3.7 *Cross another plank bridge, and continue climbing.*

4.48 *At a Y, Dacy Clearing is reachable by going in either direction. Go left, following the Longway Trail. (On your right is the Shortway Trail.)*

Signs at this point will orient you to the Upper Hogtown Parking Area. The Longway Trail is only a bit longer, and the surface is much better. Cross another bridge or two as you go.

4.9 *Arrive at a barrier and go around it into Dacy Clearing, a grassy spot at the site of an old settlement.*

Pass a couple of old foundations.

4.94 *Reaching a dirt road, across which is a very well-preserved and interesting old house foundation, turn right and head toward the Upper Hogtown Parking Area.*

6.4 *Arrive back at the parking area and your car.*

From Upper Hogtown Parking Area, a 3-mile round-trip ride can be made by heading into Dacy Clearing and going past it to the horse-trail assembly area at the Sleeping Beauty, Bumps Pond, Fishbrook Pond trailheads. Here, too, are primitive campsites and more opportunities for exploration than you might be in the mood to take advantage of. Perhaps the most alluring, and worth another day's ride, is the lakeside carriageway that runs from Black Mountain Point south past Red Rock to nearly Pearl Point, a distance of roughly 4 miles. It's testimony to the terrain that most local riders prefer to access that area by boat.

Camping Permits and General Information

Forest Ranger Headquarters: NYSDEC, Hudson Street Extension, Box 220, Warrensburg, NY 12885: 518-668-5441

Bike Shops

FlipFlop Cycle Shop, 175 Canada Street, Lake George, NY: 518-668-2233

18
Stony Creek

Location: *Warren County, Town of Stony Creek, Wilcox Lake Wild Forest*
Distance: *7.8 miles*
Terrain: *Hilly and flat sections*
Surface Conditions: *Rough dirt roads, doubletrack and singletrack trails*
Rating: *Intermediate/advanced*
Maps: *USGS: Harrisburg; ADK: Old Roads and Open Peaks of the Sacandaga Region, Trails of the Adirondack Southern Region, Eastern Region*
Highlights: *Remote camping and fishing, suspension bridges; possible thru-links to Wells; miles of surrounding trails*

This ride is considerably off the "edge" of civilization in an area of the Adirondack Park that reminds me of the fringe alpine towns of the Rockies, with clear-running rivers, rugged mountain scenery, dark pine forests, and small, wind-battered hamlets. Tin roofs bleeding rust atop dust-coated storefronts are framed within the picturesque Deer Leap Hills. Stony Creek peacefully nudges its floodplain across open meadows blinking with pastel wildflowers, languidly accepting its dissolution with the Hudson below Walnut Ridge. The feeling of removal and isolation you get in the area around Stony Creek is surprising, since it's not far from either Glens Falls, Warrensburg, or Lake George, along the southern park boundary in the Adirondack foothills, where even in June chimneys blow fragrant woodsmoke that lies in thin, misty strips over the fields of little hobby farms.

This tour will take you into the heart of the Wilcox Lake Wild Forest, a substantial swath of virgin-looking high country on the eastern flanks of the comparatively vast Siamese Ponds and Silver Lakes Wilderness

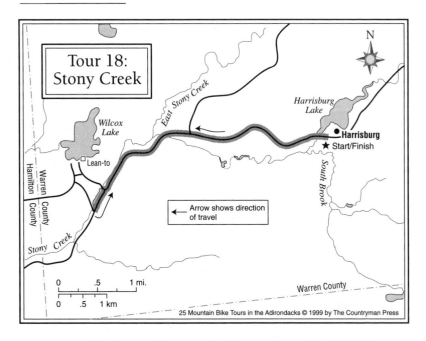

Tour 18:
Stony Creek

Wilcox
Lake

East Stony Creek

Harrisburg
Lake

●**Harrisburg**
★ Start/Finish

□ Lean-to

Warren
Hamilton

County

County

South Brook

← Arrow shows direction
of travel

Stony Creek

| 0 | .5 | 1 mi. |
| 0 | .5 | 1 km |

Warren County

25 Mountain Bike Tours in the Adirondacks © 1999 by The Countryman Press

Areas. As such, the usual caveats for being prepared with bike-repair tools, food, water, and rain gear apply. And don't forget insect repellent. If you're going in during blackfly season, you might even take a bug jacket and pants. As with all forays into the middle of nowhere, let someone know your plans or at least leave a note on your car. After the first few weeks of fishing season and until hunting season begins, there won't be too much activity in this part of the Adirondack outback.

The directions get fairly involved. To get to Stony Creek and your trailhead at Harrisburg Lake, take Exit 16 off the Adirondack Northway (I-87), and head west on CR 33 toward NY 9, setting your car's odometer to zero. Go through the intersection of NY 9, where you'll see a sign that says CORINTH, 6 MILES. Go straight on Corinth Mt. Road (CR 33). At 4.8 miles, go straight on CR 24, heading toward Corinth. International Paper is here, and you'll see decks of pulpwood next to the mill, along with increasingly attractive mountain scenery beyond it. At 8.8 miles, turn right, merging into NY 9N. Go through Corinth, keeping the Hudson River to your right, and pass Corinth Park and beach on your right. You're headed for Lake Luzerne and Hadley. At 13.8 miles, go left toward Stony Creek. At 14.3 miles, take a left onto Bridge Street, and cross the Sacandaga River at the ruggedly scenic Rockwell Falls. Now you're in Hadley. At 14.7 miles, turn right onto CR 1, and head for Stony Creek. Now you'll be driving along a great biking road with sandy shoulders of glacial till and great views to the east beyond the Hudson River. A railroad berm is up to your left. After a sign that says THE ROAD TO A FRIENDLY TOWN IS NEVER LONG, you get to Stony Creek at 24.2 miles. Continue through this funky and lovable rare find of an Adirondack frontier town, with its mountaintop and river scenery (there's a hotel, phones, and gas, but don't expect a CVS!). Go straight through town, and at 36 miles hit dirt. This is Harrisburg Lake. There's a parking area just before you get to a tiny bridge over South Brook. Park and ride.

The best thing about this trip is the trail's proximity to Stony Creek's east branch and the fine opportunities for both wilderness camping and fishing that it presents. There are wooden suspension bridges, pure pine forests, primitive campsites, and a decent, if not bumpy and rocky, old jeep trail that serves as your treadway. This is not a trail for very young or tender children, however, and even though there are no bad hills, there are some long ones, each with a good selection of stones, mud holes, and slippery ruts. Strong beginners with a sense of adventure will have no problem, though, and all other riders above that ability level will enjoy the bumps, swales, and needle-covered flats. Any hybrid with loaded panniers could make this trail, and mountain-biking touring cyclists could continue straight through to Wells to make a rather long two-day circular out of this otherwise in-out trip. Or use it as a through route to connect with the town of Speculator and the northern, established road-bike routes around Indian Lake, Blue Mountain Lake, Long Lake, and Tupper Lake. The possibilities for bikepacking, fly-fishing, and exploring in this area are great.

0.0 *From the parking lot, head west (straight ahead in the same direction you've been driving), and cross the bridge.*

Watch for an excellent spring on your left as you climb a rough dirt road.

0.1 *Bear right at the intersection of a similar dirt road, following the "main drag."*

You'll see old snowmobile signs along the way and a few hunting camps. The surface is rocky and rutted and can be a nuisance if it's been wet of late. This is no rail trail.

Into the Wilcox Lake Forest

2.1 At a trail T, signs are posted indicating Wilcox Lake, Willis Lake, and Brownell's Camp, which is in your direction of travel.

The trail to Baldwin Spring goes off to the right on a narrow, unkempt, leaf- and rock-covered surface of forest duff, a seldom-maintained snowmobile trail running along East Stony Creek and past its marshy headwaters. This is a legal bike trail, too, and is suited to the more ambitious rider with plenty of time to explore. The distance to Baldwin Spring is shown at 7.5 miles on the trail sign. The creek to your left is South Brook.

Go straight ahead downhill, toward Wilcox Lake.

Just beyond the trail signs is a primitive campsite, but there are far better ones ahead along the creek.

2.5 Arrive at a suspension bridge spanning South Brook.

This is a fine camping area, where fishermen come in the spring to camp at any of the pine-forest sites you'll see all around you. There are other deep, dark strips of maturing forest where it's possible to camp well hidden from the rest of the sites around the creek. The road surface improves now, leveling and narrowing over needle-covered dirt. You're following blue markers.

3.0 At a point near an oxbow in Stony Creek, you'll come upon the Moosewood Hunting Club's cabin.

You won't see the oxbow from the road unless you take a short trail that leads to it on your right, just as you first see the cabin. This trail is ridable and short, and it will give you a fine look at the creek and the mountains beyond, where the water funnels down across beaver dams from the high country toward Wolf Point. The Moosewood Club has private holdings in this area, and the little posted trails around it that serve as their hunting access roads should be avoided. It appears certain that the signs are directed toward the four-wheeling hunting and fishing public, who have contributed severely to the impact throughout the area. You'll ride through the ruts and potholes they've created here, where many small side trails go around the deeper mudholes. Around the holes, this section is fast and smooth. Pine forests continue, and rocks diminish within a shining balsam woods.

3.6 Arrive at a fording spot on your right, which leads to Wilcox

Lake Lean-to and the lake itself (elevation 1,445'). Don't ford here, but keep going straight.

The jeep roads to the lake are steep, rocky, and washed out but not impossible to ride for the true enthusiast. It's easy to ford here through about a foot or more of Stony Creek and make a loop to Wilcox Lake, returning on the next trail south, just north of Wilcox Mountain. However, ahead is a bridge you may prefer to use.

3.9 *On reaching a T, you'll see the suspension bridge on your left.*

A trail sign here shows Wilcox Lake to the right at 0.7 mile and Willis Lake at 5 miles. Brownell Camp is straight ahead, at an estimated distance of 3 or 4 miles. Just across the bridge is a primitive little campsite, right on the edge of Stony Creek—your turn-around point. The hike to Wilcox Lake requires a 300-foot elevation gain, and is not easily ridable. A marked trail from the lake, which at times crosses Wilcox Outlet, leads to Willis Lake and Pumpkin Hollow in the town of Wells and is within an easy distance of the Sacandaga Public Campsite.

As you sway on the suspension bridge, surveying the lively creek below, you're going to wish you'd brought along your tent and fishing pole, particularly in the early spring, when pan-sized trout are easily beguiled with the right fly and a bit of patience.

Return the way you came.

Camping Permits and General Information

Forest Ranger Headquarters: NYSDEC, Hudson Street Extension, Box 220, Warrensburg, NY 12885: 518-668-5441

Bike Shops

Inside Edge Ski and Bike Shop, 624 Upper Glen Road (NY 9), Glens Falls, NY: 518-793-5676

The Bike Shop, 368 Ridge Road (corner of Ridge and and Quaker Roads), Glens Falls, NY: 518-793-8986

FlipFlop Cycle Shop, 175 Canada Street, Lake George, NY: 518-668-2233

19
Warren County Bikeway:
Lake George to Glens Falls

Location: *Warren County, connecting Lake George and Glens Falls*
Terrain: *Gently rolling*
Distance: *9.6 miles round-trip*
Surface conditions: *Paved bikeway, minimal road travel*
Rating: *Beginner*
Map: *Warren County Bikeway Area Map, available from Warren County*
Parks and Recreation Division, Dept. of Public Works, Warrensburg,
NY 12885, 518-623-4141; partially shown on The Adirondacks: Lake
George Region map and on Warren County maps.
Highlights: *Mountain scenery; woodlands; ideal beginner route; Lake*
George Beach State Park; Battleground Public Campground

This is the village of Lake George's showcase bike path. It leaves near the towns Million Dollar Beach and is the most popular exercise trail in the area. Even if you're not staying in Lake George, and especially if you've never been there, this ride is justified by the scenery from Million Dollar Beach alone.

Although it can't be said that Lake George has a great number of mountain-bike trails, a few special rides will keep the errant vacationer satisfied. Local cyclists or those visiting Warren County to explore the extensive scenic rides in the area will find a variety of routes at all ability levels. In addition to attractive county roads, mountain bikers can ride the undeveloped trails around Shelving Rock (see Tour #17), Silver Bay, Jabe Pond, and other northerly destinations that are described in hand-outs you can get at FlipFlop Bicycle Shop. Gary Filipelli, the shop's owner, is doing most of the regional trail advocacy at this time, and as of this writing he's preparing to designate 5 kilometers of what will

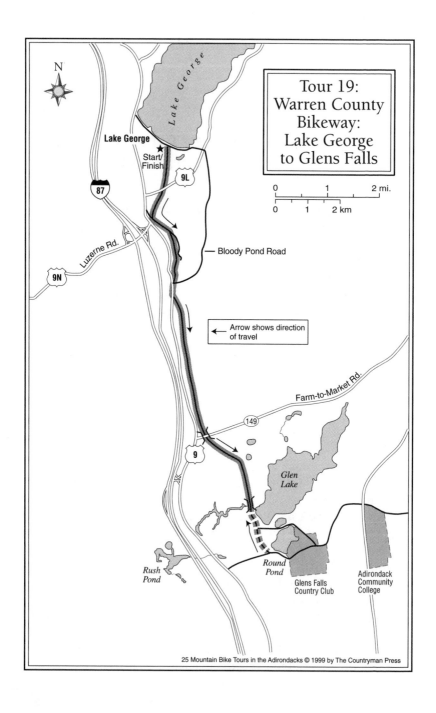

N

Lake George

Lake George

Start/Finish

87

9L

Luzerne Rd.

9N

Bloody Pond Road

Tour 19:
Warren County
Bikeway:
Lake George
to Glens Falls

0   1   2 mi.

0   1   2 km

← Arrow shows direction
of travel

Farm-to-Market Rd.

149

9

Glen
Lake

Rush
Pond

Round
Pond

Glens Falls
Country Club

Adirondack
Community
College

eventually become 40–60 kilometers of singletrack on the Lake George Recreation Center's lands. He can help you find the place—and other good rides nearby. And you can get the Warren County free handout, *Mountain Biking Trails,* from the Warren County Tourism Office (see information at the end of this tour). This mimeographed publication contains carbon copies of routes described in the Preliminary Trail and Route Listing (ADK). It also has information about the Glens Falls Feeder Canal Trail in addition to the Warren County Bikeway. The Feeder Canal linear park and bike trail, which can be enjoyed by both mountain and touring cyclists, can be reached by riding south on the Warren County Bikeway and going through Glens Falls. It's best to drive there, unless you're up for a long ride (see information at the end of this tour).

Rated a beginner route because it's paved and gently contoured, the Warren County Bikeway has attributes any cyclist would appreciate. Campers from Lake George toting tag-a-longs and child seats, pedestrians with baby joggers, and neighborhood kids on foot and bikes comprise most of its users. This is the ultimate ride-to-the-beach tour if you start in Glens Falls and is the ideal break from camp for those vacationing in Lake George. An easy out-and-back tour of just under 10 miles can be managed in two relaxed hours.

To reach the bikeway from Glens Falls, get off the Adirondack Northway (I-87) at Exit 19. Turn east (right, if you're heading north) on Aviation Road (NY 254). At 0.6 mile, cross US 9. Aviation Road becomes Quaker Road. Continue east on Quaker Road for 0.6 mile, turn left on Country Club Road, go 0.3 mile, and park at the Warren County Bike Path parking area. A few picnic tables dot this wooded lot.

To reach the bikeway from Lake George, get off at either Exit 21 or Exit 22 of the Adirondack Northway (I-87), and head for the village. Along NY 9 (Canada Street) in the middle of the village get on Beach Road, which follows directly along the edge of the lake's south shore. This is Lake George Beach State Park. The view to the north is tremendous. Cruise out past Fort William Henry on your right, and park on the first road to your right, which will be West Brook Road. On your left at this point is the Battleground Public Campground. The bikeway starts here, on the paved surface you'll see leading into the woods through the park. (Though you can't see any tents or campers from this point, the beach and campground form one large entity of grassy lawn and beach environment.) You'll see a large sign telling you this is the bike path.

The views from this point are impressive, containing an approximately 35-mile panorama of lake and mountains to the north. Peaks in excess of 2,000 feet are numerous to the east. Several lower peaks are to the north beyond North Bolton and Northwest Bay, and Prospect Mountain is to the west (left).

0.0 *Head south on the bike path, going easily uphill, and ride through lands of the Battleground Campground.*

If you're going to let small children go ahead, tell them to wait for you at each stop sign or not to get out of sight of you. There are some crossroads and mergers.

0.7 *Cross over NY 9L (American Legion Drive).*

0.97 *Cross a small private road (stop sign).*

1.1 *Reaching Old Military Road, the bikeway follows it. Stay to your right.*

Within 500 feet, the bikeway leaves the road again.

1.9 *The trail parallels NY 9 near Magic Forest Amusement Park.*

Observe stop signs as you cross Bloody Pond Road, find the path on the other side, and drift downhill now through a pine forest over gently rolling terrain.

4.0 *Cross over NY 149 on a fun, arched wooden bridge.*

4.7 *Following a nice downhill run, cross Glen Lake Road amid honeysuckled woodlands.*

4.8 *Cross Ash Drive, and pull out onto a wooden bridge over the outlet of Glen Lake.*

There are views of the Luzerne Mountains from here, beyond Glen Lake swamp (Darling, 1,850'; Bucktail, 1,837'; Bartlett, 1,540').

This is a logical turn-around point, although the bikeway continues to another pretty spot just ahead, at 5 miles (uphill), next to Round Pond. After that the path becomes increasingly busy and enters suburban Glens Falls. It continues with some dull road mileage to the Glens Falls Country Club, past the Bay Meadows Golf Course, and ends at Adirondack Community College for an additional 4 miles. Riders wishing to access the Feeder Canal Trail can do so by proceeding from Round Pond, turning left onto Round Pond Road, and staying on the bikeway until Bay Road (CR 7) is

The Warren County Bikeway's northern entrance, Lake George

reached. Turning right, follow Bay Road onto NY 9, and pick up Oakland Avenue on the left, just before crossing the river. Proceed one mile to Warren Street, turn right, turn right again onto Shermantown Road, cross over the canal and take a left onto the towpath. The total distance from Round Pond is about 3.5 miles. Once on the towpath at this location, you can go approximately 5 miles in either direction. The right (west) is the more scenic of the two choices. A designated road connection is planned for these bike paths.

Though the tourist appeal of Lake George itself can prove overwhelming, a ride through the streets among the many eateries and souvenir shops is an experience made easy on a bicycle. Contact the local chamber of commerce or stop at the information booth at Blais Lakefront Park (left on Beach Road, there are phones and restrooms here) for a list of local highlights and activities.

Return the way you came.

Information

Warren County Tourism, Municipal Center, 1340 State Route 9, Lake George, NY 12845-9803: 518-761-6366; Web site: http://www.adirondacks.org/lakegeorge

Feeder Canal Alliance, PO Box 2414, Glens Falls, NY 12801: 518-792-5363

Bicycle Shops

Inside Edge Ski and Bike Shop, 624 Upper Glen Road (NY 9), Glens Falls, NY: 518-793-5676

The Bike Shop, 368 Ridge Road (corner of Ridge and and Quaker Roads), Glens Falls, NY: 518-793-8986

FlipFlop Cycle Shop, 175 Canada Street, Lake George, NY: 518-668-2233

IV. CENTRAL MOUNTAINS

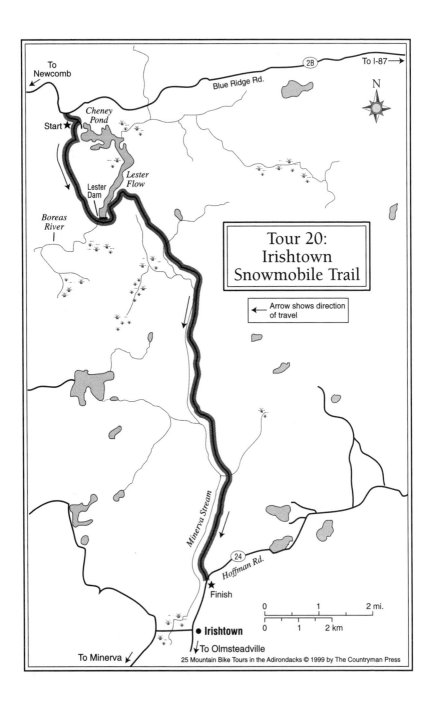

To
Newcomb

2B

To I-87 →

Blue Ridge Rd.

N

*Cheney
Pond*

Start ★

*Lester
Flow*

Lester
Dam

*Boreas
River*

Tour 20:
Irishtown
Snowmobile Trail

← Arrow shows direction
of travel

Minerva Stream

24

Hoffman Rd.

★
Finish

| 0 | | 1 | | 2 mi. |

| 0 | 1 | | 2 km |

● **Irishtown**

↓ To Olmsteadville

To Minerva ↙

25 Mountain Bike Tours in the Adirondacks © 1999 by The Countryman Press

20
Irishtown Snowmobile Trail

Location: *Hamilton County, Town of Minerva, Vanderwhacker Mountain Wild Forest*
Terrain: *Hilly, wilderness atmosphere*
Distance: *13 dirt miles, one way; 21 miles return by road; total, 34 miles*
Surface conditions: *Doubletrack, singletrack, stream fordings, mud, rocks, blowdowns*
Rating: *Advanced*
Maps: *The Adirondacks: Lake George Region, Central Mountains (for road details); USGS: Schroon Lake, Dutton Mountain; ADK: Central Region*
Highlights: *Rugged backcountry; technical singletrack; overnight camping; can be combined with road miles*

This tour is recommended only to strong, highly advanced and experienced riders who are well equipped and prepared for a demanding, technical outing. Whiners will suffer egregiously. The trail begins innocently enough on a wide, grassy section of snowmobile trail to Lester Dam (this section is fine for beginners), but beyond the dam it changes radically into a narrow, rocky, hill-ridden singletrack followed by many choice miles of large rocks and mud puddles, all of it punctuated with blowdowns, deadfalls, boggy mires, and sometimes deeper-than-you'd-like-to-bike stream fordings. For the uninitiated ATBer used to carriage roads and flat, friendly neighborhood tours, this trail will seem a bad joke. This is the Adirondack backcountry in all its mush and splendor, forming the rugged western boundary of the Hoffman Notch Wilderness Area, complete with moose traffic. Be careful and plan accordingly. Gelpaks, food, bug repellent, water, tubes, and tools are mandatory, and don't go without eye protection and your helmet. A visor may prove useful. You get the picture?

Logistics for this tour are problematic, requiring some planning and flexibility. For starters, it is without question preferable to ride southward, taking advantage of the considerable elevation loss (about a 700-foot drop over 13 miles) that will enable you to "glide" the technical stuff. Local riders beginning in Minerva and Olmsteadville by virtue of their locations ride in from the south (part way) for convenience sake, since for them the trailhead is 21 miles away, doing in-out tours that may be recommended to you from people in those locations (do not yield!). To see the whole trail adequately—and to do so logically and comfortably, maximizing the ride's inherent pleasures—through-cyclers are better off arranging for a pickup or dropping a shuttle car at the southern terminus. This will save you the 21-mile return to the northern trailhead. While 21 miles doesn't sound like a great deal of distance to most serious cyclists, the combination of road (uphill) and wilderness miles adds up to more than you may have bargained for. Get an early start! The potential for carrying a bivy sack and a light sleeping bag makes this trail a good candidate for bikepacking. By all means stop in at Kindred Spirits Outfitters (see the info at the end of the chapter), and talk to Rick Beardsley, the most knowledgeable guide in the area. He'll have some ideas about logistical planning, the maps you'll need, and information about existing trail conditions.

The tour begins at the Cheney Pond Trailhead, about 8 miles east of Newcomb on NY 2B (Blue Ridge Road), which forks off of NY 28N, 0.5 mile east of Newcomb. Coming from the east, the trailhead is 13 miles west of Exit 29 off the Adirondack Northway (I-87). An ideal staging point for getting an early start is the Harris Lake State Campground in Newcomb, and camping is also permitted near the trailhead within a short distance of the parking area (Cheney Pond, primitive and not patrolled). Camping is, of course, also available in the forest preserve itself, and there are several other areas along the highway where it's legal to pull over and pitch a tent or trailer camp if you look around a bit. Just make sure that you're parked legally and that you camp at least 150 feet back from the road.

Park at the Cheney Pond Trailhead access parking area. A signpost at the trailhead reads: CHENEY POND, 1 MILE; LESTER DAM, 2.5 MILES; AND IRISHTOWN TRAILHEAD VIA HOFFMAN ROAD, 11 MILES.

0.0 *Descend from the parking area*

0.7 *Pass the snowmobile trail on your right.*

This is your route, but it's worth a ride down to the pond for a look.

0.9 *Arrive at the shore of Cheney Pond for a fair view or to camp.*

This isn't the greatest camping location, however. Somebody has an RV encamped there in the summer months, and it spoils it for everybody else.

Turn around and backtrack uphill.

1.1 *Turn left onto the snowmobile trail, posted with snowmobile signs.*

3.16 *Pass through a boggy area where wild iris blooms.*

The trail is grass and pine-needle covered beyond, traveling gently downhill through a heavily wooded area.

3.5 *You will hear the flowing Boreas River before you arrive at the edge of Lester Flow.*

Beginners can come to this point comfortably, making for a fine in-out tour. Look carefully and you'll spot the red snowmobile signs and the trail's location on the east bank. If the signs are no longer visible, proceed across the stream at its narrowest point, where you'll find the old log abutments of Lester Dam. Be careful here, where the flow runs between the narrows. The water can be powerful enough to sweep you off your feet. Ford at a sensible place, taking care not to submerge your bottom bracket, which will considerably speed up the death-by-rust of your bike's precious bearings. Watch it on the slippery rocks, too, especially if you're carrying a camera or other nonsubmersibles, and go easy to ward off an ankle or shin injury. In the summer, you're going to get wet up to your knees, and in the spring, the water may be crotch deep. Consider carrying sneakers and dry socks or sandals for the fording. (In any event, your pedaling footwear will most likely get wet ahead, in Minerva Stream.) And prospects for fording farther downstream from here are poor, since the flow widens again and thereafter becomes boggy. This is it!

The trail proceeds on the east bank as if it were a continuation of the road that once crossed the dam.

You'll find snowmobile signs at length, even if you have to search around, emanating from an outcropping of moss-laden bedrock. Regroup here, as it's much nicer than the west bank and maybe less buggy. Views upriver (north) on the flow take in the high peaks and a wide panorama of nameless hills and mountains. Strap down and tie in your loose gear here as ravens *grokk* overhead.

Sashaying around innumerable red efts (salamanders) amid elegant Atlantic white cedars, follow the thin singletrack embroidered by ferns and wildflowers, and head for the boonies. Brush against balsam and vagrant stems of hawkweed as you climb. You'll inevitably encounter a few blowdowns now, many of which will sport the deep, reassuring chain-ring gashes of those who have gone before you.

4.57 Encounter a sign that says STATE LAND WILDERNESS AREA.

This is the eastern fringe of the Hoffman Notch Wilderness Area, about as close as you can legally get to riding in an Adirondack Wilderness Area.

4.87 Cross a mushy, 2-foot-wide creek.

Marking is good, and the trail is self-guiding. Markers vary in composition and condition. Some are homemade, others peppered with shot.

6.06 Ford Minerva Stream.

There are a lot of skinny, shin-high blowdowns through here. Watch those sharp branches on you and your bike. Just across the stream is an old tin marker that a disgruntled hunter splattered with bird shot. The trail becomes more difficult now, sporting rocks, hummocky soil, roots, an uneven treadway, and pools of water. You'll be on foot frequently. Cross some very old, beat-up corduroy where the forest is so dense, even the moose are using the trail—or drinking out of it.

7.06 Cross the stream again.

It's about 10 feet wide and running briskly here.

7.37 Ford again in an even livelier—but not too deep—section of Minerva Stream.

A cable is strung across the creek here, probably for hiker safety during the spring thaw. The trail improves after this section of creek.

8.20 *After following the creek for a while, on your left pass a beaver pond where wild iris blooms. Cross an outlet and continue on the trail.*

8.26 *You arrive at a charming log-cabin hunting camp. Pass right by the front door, descending slightly.*

8.41 *Across the stream you'll see another, more upscale, cabin.*

The trail can be remarkably muddy and rocky here, and to classify it as technical would be moot. Just slog it. The brook has risen above the trail in places. You can't ride for extended periods, but mosquitoes are fierce and unrelenting when you walk. Remount when you are able. The trail improves; the flies don't.

8.5 *Ford Minerva Stream again, climbing away from it to drier ground.*

All the topsoil is washed off the trail here, suggesting that the stream rises to its level during thaw.

9.0 *The trail gains in elevation.*

Rocks persist in mind-boggling numbers. This is some of the best rock-hopping you ever saw, but be prepared to dodge deep, beefy mudholes (if you still have a clean spot on your body). Very pretty riding through here.

11.3 *Cross a gravelly tributary to Minerva Stream.*

You can rinse your feet here. Pass a few trailer camps, an ugly old bus, and some junk.

13.5 *Pull out on the road after a long, flat run.*

Pass a legitimate residence on your right. Just before the Y intersection of the road you're on (the continuation of the snowmobile trail) and Shelvin Road, which comes in on the right, you'll see a state snowmobile trail sign posted, almost hidden by the bushes on your right. It reads: BLUE MOUNTAIN HIGHWAY 11M, VIA MINERVA STREAM AND LESTER DAM.

It's about 21 miles by road back to the trailhead, so let's hope you've planned for a shuttle. Don't ignore the possibilities for camping. Whatever you do, you probably won't want to turn around to retrace your route, but it is *possible*. To get back to your car up at the Cheney Pond trailhead by bike the easiest way, bear right at the next fork onto CR 24, at 1.2 miles turn right in Irishtown (barely distinguishable), leaving St. Mary's Church to your right and crossing a small wetlands, then go left at 2 miles, and pass Minerva Lake. Turn right into Minerva, and then go north (uphill, remember) on NY 28N, cranking the 13 miles to Blue Ridge Road; turn right (east), and go 5 more miles back to the Cheney trailhead. Thank God that's over!

Camping Permits and General Information

Forest Ranger Headquarters: NYSDEC, 701 South Main Street, Box 458, Northville, NY 12134: 518-863-4545

Bike Shop and Information Center

Kindred Spirits Adirondack Outfitters, Four Corners, Olmsteadville, NY: 518-251-5131; 1-800-799-HIKE; e-mail: kindred@netheaven.com.

21
Camp Santanoni

Location: *Essex County, Town of Newcomb, Santanoni Preserve*
Terrain: *Gently rolling*
Distance: *10 miles round-trip*
Surface Conditions: *Wide gravel road*
Maps: *The Adirondacks: High Peaks Region; USGS: Newcomb, Santanoni Peak*
Rating: *Beginner/intermediate*
Highlights: *Tour an Adirondack Great Camp; excellent family outing suitable for totes and tag-a-longs; views of Adirondack High Peaks; convenient to Harris Lake State Campground and Public Day-Use Area; nearby Adirondack Visitor Interpretive Center*

This "showpiece" tour is an easy but substantial ride—with only one long hill—into the densely forested and very attractive terrain lying due south of the Santanoni Mountains (Little Santanoni, Couchsachraga, Panther, and the dominating Santanoni, at elevation 4,607'), all of them members of the High Peaks Wilderness Area. You get a good, close look at the entire range plus dozens of other High Peaks from various areas around Newcomb, most notably from the town's picnic and rest area, which is situated a short distance east of the Santanoni Preserve entrance on NY 28N. A very cleverly designed plexiglass view sign details the High Peaks skyline and is an interpretive aid to identifying the peaks. You stand in front of the sign, align your vision to connect the real ridge line with the one on the plexiglass, and you can pick out each individual peak, at least in theory. Another kind of interesting spot—though not a great view—is about a half mile down the hill from the rest area at the Hudson River Information Center, indicated by signs, where a small building shelters an interpretive kiosk on the river's edge.

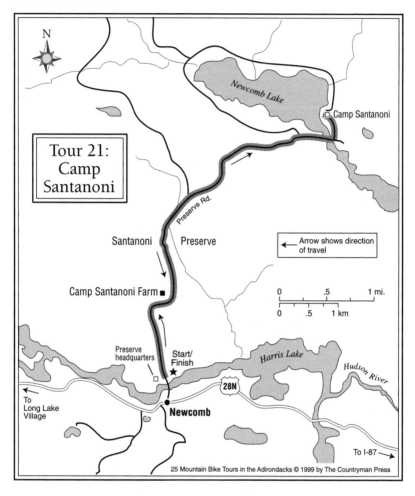

You will find the Santanoni Preserve 13.5 miles east of Long Lake Village on NY 28N or west about a 25-mile drive from Exit 29 of the Adirondack Northway (I-87). Just as you start heading west off the exit there's a beautiful (unmarked but obvious, on the left) place to pull over and check out the Boreas River, which flows close to the road here. Continuing west, follow Blue Ridge Road (amazed by its unbelievable scenery) as it joins NY 28N (you're really going west). Set your odometer to zero as you cross the Hudson River. Just on the west side of Newcomb you'll see the signs for the Preserve on your right at 1.9 miles;

turn right here. If you reach the Adirondack Visitor Interpretive Center, you've gone exactly 1 mile too far west.

Because the Preserve road is meticulously maintained and patrolled, this is an excellent tour for single or family cyclists who are most comfortable in more secure settings. But it is still a wilderness (technically, it is "wild forest"), and anyone venturing forth on this road should be both mechanically and mentally prepared. The road is graded and open to horses, horse-drawn carriages, state maintenance vehicles (which you probably won't encounter), pedestrians, and cyclists. It's a popular spot, and especially on a weekend you'll encounter many other trail users. If you bring younger children on this tour, come suitably equipped with rain gear, insect repellent, and lots of snacks to keep morale high. Not that you shouldn't bring such things for yourselves—it's just easier for adults to run from disagreeable situations at this relatively short distance, while children have a determined pace. Tandem hybrids, tote bikes, tag-a-long child carriers, and even well-shod touring bikes with sturdy, wide-bead tires have made this trip, but hybrids and mountain bikes are most at home on the loose gravel and dirt surface.

The attraction here is not only in the quality of the ride itself—which winds through deep and alluring forests and across the pellucid narrows and shores of Newcomb Lake, with its enchanting, typically Adirondack texture. You also get to visit and (if a resident guide is on hand) even tour Camp Santanoni itself, which was built on the shore of Newcomb Lake in 1892 and is still largely intact and becoming increasingly accessible to the public. The central camp consists of six buildings covered by one roof, plus a huge porch with absolutely ostentatious views. This is the prime splendor and luxury of another time, and the presently weathered though structurally intact main camp is being continually restored with your tax dollars and assorted other funds, many more of which are needed. I'm sure you'll agree that your tax money has been wisely appropriated as you sit on the porch and wonder what the place must have been like in the heyday of the Adirondack Great Camp era. For a brief history of the place, get a copy of Howard Kirschenbaum's essay, appropriately entitled "A Brief History of Camp Santanoni," which is distributed by the Preserve staff and represents a piece of the historic site's interpretive efforts.

Park in the designated area and get oriented. There are pit privies near the parking area and at the Great Camp.

0.0 *Head for Great Camp and Newcomb Lake, which are indicated on a sign at the trailhead, at a distance of 5 miles.*

Moose Pond is also shown, but you can't go there by bike, since it's wilderness. To the right at this trailhead you will also see signs to Lake Harris Public Campground at NY 28; the trail is legal, but challenging.

Go straight through the gate, heading north, leaving the old gatehouse to your right.

Here you are greeted by more trail signs, which designate locations within the Wilderness Area.

0.5 *A nameless wetland materializes into a small creek to your right.*

1.0 *Arrive at the camp's farm complex, which has a gorgeous barn and some good views to the northeast.*

Here you're traveling easily uphill, then riding flat, through a mixed hardwood and balsam forest, over a wide sandy surface. You'll have to be in fairly good shape to pull a tag-a-long—though you can always walk! But the hills are not strenuous.

2.1 *Cross a bridge with stone railings.*

2.43 *Arrive at a Y, and bear right toward Newcomb Lake.*

The left fork is the departure road for interior wilderness sites such as Moose Pond, Shattuck Clearing, Calkin's Creek, and fabled interior locations like the Cold River, haunt of the hermit Noah John Rondeau, as well as a piece of the Northville–Lake Placid Trail to Millers Falls and Duck Hole. Unless you want to hike this access road sometime, you're going to have to "get a horse." These are some of the finest, most desirable (but muddy) equestrian trails anywhere. Don't ever let a horse person tell you they're getting the short shrift by having to share any trails with bikes, but do stop and dismount while riders pass. It's common decency and accepted IMBA protocol.

4.3 *After coasting the previous mile, you begin to get a look at the lake as you pass a camp and picnic site on your left just before crossing the Newcomb Lake narrows.*

This is a great spot to linger, and there are several other spots in which to do so lavishly. There are picnic tables around.

Long Lake, west of Newcomb

4.4   Cross the bridge.

4.9   Arrive at the main camp.

There are walking trails here, and most times there's an intern from Adirondack Architectural Heritage who will happily show you around the grounds and buildings. Here, too, are a few privies.

A total of 8 campsites are on Newcomb Lake. Tenting up to 3 days without a permit is allowed. Fishing is also legal, but only with worms and artificial lures. Live bait is prohibited, from fear that undesirable species of fish might infiltrate the lake.

Newcomb Lake is fed by Santanoni and Sucker Brooks, which come in from the north, off of the southern slopes of the Santanoni Peaks. The lake itself drains into the Newcomb River and finally into the Hudson in nearby Winebrook. This is wild country at its best—and at its worst. For the saga of Santanoni ends on a tragic note, with the story of young Douglas Legg, the 8-year-old grandson of one of Santanoni's later owners. In 1971 he wandered off and was never seen again, his disappearance spurring the state's largest wilderness search-and-rescue operation to date. Heartbroken, and unable to bear remaining at the location of the tragedy, the family sold the estate to The Nature Conservancy, who then resold it to New York State.

You might reflect on this incident and on the silent power of the wilderness while you admire the majestic, hypnotic peaks. Keep your little ones near, perhaps giving them whistles and instructions about what you want them to do should they become lost themselves.

Retrace your path back to headquarters.

Camping Permits and General Information

Forest Ranger Headquarters: NYSDEC, Route 86, Box 296, Ray Brook, NY 12977-0296: 518-897-1200

Bike Shop and Information Center

Kindred Spirits Adirondack Outfitters, Four Corners, Olmsteadville, NY: 518-251-5131; 1-800-799-HIKE; e-mail: kindred@netheaven.com.

V. HIGH PEAKS REGION

22
Styles Brook

Location: *Essex County, Towns of Jay and Lewis, near Jay Primitive Area*
Terrain: *Steep hills, high country flats*
Distance: *20 miles round-trip*
Surface Conditions: *Dirt roads*
Rating: *Advanced*
Maps: *The Adirondacks: High Peaks Region; USGS: Keene and Jay; Essex County road map; ADK: High Peaks Region*
Highlights: *Excellent views; challenging terrain; high, exposed conditions; extraordinary hills*

Here's one tour that will blow your mind, maybe your tubes, but definitely your socks off. I found its description in a handout at High Peaks Cyclery in Lake Placid, under the name "Fear and Loathing," which is apt. I suspect it's the most demanding tour in the book, at least insofar as personal fitness goes. It's not technical, and any beginner could ride the surfaces, but it's high, it's removed, and it's pure hills. The place names are ominous as well—you'll be in the company of Seths Hill, Big Slash, and Death and Bitch Mountains, for starters. Once you top out onto the high alpine meadows between Clements Mountain and the Soda Range, however, you won't be thinking of slasher movies. Instead you'll be annoying your friends and family by whistling intentionally off-tune renditions of the *Sound of Music*. Even if you're not a Maria Von Trapp type, you'll be amazed and enthralled by the incredible views of the Sentinel Range, the High Peaks Wilderness, and the surrounding up-close nubs and ridges of the scraggly, wind-ravaged Hurricane and Jay Mountain Primitive Areas. A great deal of return-trip planning and various shuttle arrangements will be left to your creative imagination here, making their appeal as you peruse the High Peaks Wilderness Area Map. Because of

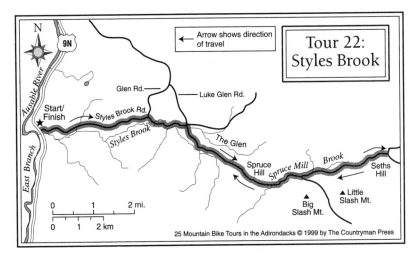

N
9N

Arrow shows direction of travel

Tour 22:
Styles Brook

Glen Rd.
Luke Glen Rd.

Start/
Finish
Styles Brook Rd.

Styles Brook

The Glen

Spruce
Hill
Spruce Mill Brook
Seths
Hill

Auerable River

East Branch

Little
Slash Mt.

Big
Slash Mt.

0   1   2 mi.
0   1   2 km

25 Mountain Bike Tours in the Adirondacks © 1999 by The Countryman Press

the relatively large distances between ingress and egress points, out-and-back approaches to touring the area will be tempting from a purely practical standpoint. The tour described herein is a popular one with extreme cyclists, emanating from the world-class fitness and recreation center in Lake Placid. But you don't have to be an Olympian to pedal a good deal of this sacred ground, and even if you never bike it at all, it would be a shame to miss out on the views from the flats north of Oak Ridge, where brilliant wildflowers popping up in vast green fields amid large farms suggest the soul-cleansing character of the Swiss Alps.

This tour begins on Styles Brook Road, which is marked by a regular street sign and easily found from either Keene or Jay. Neither town is too far from Wilmington or Lake Placid to provide a convenient day outing. Find Styles Brook Road 3 miles north of Keene on NY 9N on the right, and about 2.6 miles south of Upper Jay, just past a town picnic area on the east side of NY 9N if you're coming south.

Take note, on your map, of the roads just a short way from Keene, to the northwest, which more or less surround the Bark Eater Cross-Country Ski Area (Lacy, Alstead, Bartlett, and Limekiln Roads). These roads, which are tame in comparison to where you're heading, are promoted in all kinds of local and regional mountain biking literature on account of their scenery and easy ridability. If you get cold feet on the Styles Brook route, these roads make a great alternative. If you've got family with you, and your speed of travel is determined by a slower

The flats north of Oak Ridge (Styles Brook Road)

beginner, the Bark Eater roads are your best bet. You can drive them and have a look around. The roads are accessible off NY 9N, going toward Upper Jay from Keene, and north off of NY 73, heading west out of Keene. There's generally a lot going on around here. You're not far from the Mt. Van Hoevenberg Cross-Country Ski Area and its mountain biking trails, or from Whiteface Mountain, where you can ride the lifts and bike the ski trails.

Find a place to park somewhere. You can park at the picnic area just north of Styles Brook Road and ride back on NY 9N, which is a very short distance. I won't lie to you—once you hit the road, you've got a killer climb ahead of you. In the parlance of road racers, this one's a "heartbreak hill." You're looking at a 700-foot elevation gain in the next 2 miles. Saddle up, gear down, and go.

0.0 Head up Styles Brook Road. Climb.

1.9 The pavement ends in a high meadow.

It is ridiculously and overwhelmingly scenic right here. You might laugh a little and go, "Oh, wow!" It's that good. The road is wide and well maintained. This is a very good place for an alternate starting point for those who don't want the climb. I actually changed into shorts here, and nobody noticed (not that they would ordinarily). There's no place to pull over, really, but it's fine to just stop on the road and get set up if you're getting a lift. You won't encounter a great deal of traffic, I don't think.

2.9 At a Y, bear right. There are no signs here presently.

3.0 At another Y, bear left. A dead-end sign is to the left.

3.1 Cross a bridge over Styles Brook.

A private residence is on the right. You'll see signs for the town of Jay and Styles Brook Road.

3.9 Pass a couple of residences.

4.0 Reach a paved road. On the right (your route!), a seasonal limited-use sign is posted, as well as a ROAD CLOSED sign. Go right here, and proceed uphill on dirt.

If you were to turn left here—where the views are again very good—you could do a loop, turning left on Glen Road where Luke Glen Road heads downhill, and, climbing again, returning to the unsigned Y that you passed at 2.9 miles, then coming back to your current location for an extra 3.5 mile warm-up. No? So, take a right and go.

Go over a bridge.

There's no formal maintenance on this road, but there are homes on it, and it's in pretty good shape. The surface is hard-packed dirt, sand, and gravel.

4.6 A few houses appear.

5.4 The surface gets rougher and may be washed out somewhat in places, but it's still easily negotiated.

Wilderness closes in, you gain in elevation—you're at 2,300 feet—and you begin to enter the real boonies up around Spruce Hill. You'll see a few unmarked side trails here and there. Who knows where they may lead?

6.0 You get to travel along on the flats for a while.

Soon you'll go through a wet, flat area where beavers have been working hard to flood the thoroughfare by damming the headwaters of Spruce Mill Brook. You may have to slog it here a bit in wet periods when the beaver pond backs up across the road. Don't fret—you can rock-hop it. This is a good roadbed, otherwise, but of course four-wheelers have helped to rut and erode it into mush.

7.2 Cross a tiny creek.

This is dense forest. There are no views.

7.5 Descend!

Heading east, downhill now, the road improves to hard sand, but soft spots abound, so watch your speed. The elevation loss is so radical that your speed will be determined only by your nerve—and your discretion. This isn't a good place for a bad spill if you're ever going to have one. The sand gets to be a menace in spots, the road winds, and there are large boulders and ditches off to the sides as well as a few unannounced big bumps in the road. Spruce Mill Brook persists on your left.

10.0 At a T, you've reached your turn-around point.

You'll see a one-lane bridge sign to the left. This left goes out to NY 9, which you would reach at about 10.6 miles. To the right, the road heads southeast. Go this way if you're planning to ride back to the point of ingress via NY 9N, a not-too-unbearable distance of 20 hilly road miles. You would accomplish this by setting to zero and going right at the 9.9-mile T, turning left at Goff Road (0.7 mile), and right at a T at 1.8 miles, arriving at NY 9N just north of Lewis at 2.8 miles. Only another 1.4 miles ahead (east) is Exit 32 on the Adirondack Northway (I-87).

Camping Permits and General Information

Forest Ranger Headquarters: NYSDEC, Route 86, Box 296, Ray Brook, NY 12977-0296: 518-897-1200

Bike Shops

High Peaks Cyclery, 331 Main Street, Lake Placid, NY: 518-523-3764; Web site: www.hpmac.com

Placid Planet Bicycles, 200 Saranac Ave, Lake Placid, NY: 518-523-4128

23
Pine Pond

Location: *Essex County, Village of Lake Placid, Saranac Lakes Wild Forest*
Distance: *15 miles round-trip*
Terrain: *Mostly flat to rolling; one big hill*
Surface Conditions: *Dirt road, eroded in spots; smooth singletrack; some rocks and mud*
Rating: *Intermediate*
Maps: *The Adirondacks: High Peaks Region; USGS: Lake Placid, Saranac Lake*
Highlights: *Near Lake Placid; ends at a clean wilderness pond with great campsites and a sand beach*

No mountain bike book about the Adirondacks would be complete without including this exquisite ride. It is firmly in the intermediate range but would serve well as a "first-time-out-back" trip for those riders who are ready to cross that daunting line between "green" and "seasoned." I encountered several highly skilled and fully equipped riders on this trail, mounted on state-of-the-art bikes, wearing backpack hydrators. One of them was a professional team rider and factory rep. All of them had big smiles on their faces and the same general comment about the trail: "Great ride!" This is probably the best "serious" mountain biking in the immediate area.

Any bike shop in town will also have something to say about Pine Pond, plus useful information about recent trail conditions. It is often the case that you will meet someone in the shops who has ridden the trail within the last few days (or right before their shift).

Pine Pond lies near the confluence of the Saranac River and Oseetah Lake, in the pond-dotted Saranac Lakes Wild Forest area. The area is

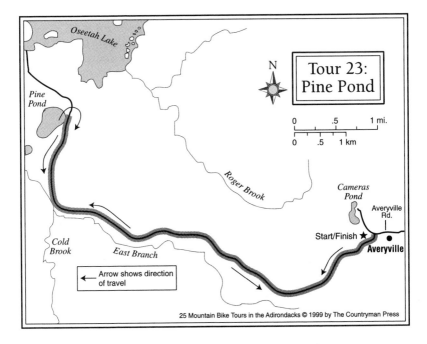

characterized by deep woods, brooks, huge lakes, and elevations averaging 1,500-plus feet. The terminus of this trail, at Pine Pond, is remote, although it is close at hand to Oseetah Lake, where egress is only possible by boat with advance arrangement—a detail that doesn't seem practical for most out-of-town riders. You may run into people who have hiked or carried canoes in from either Oseetah itself or from the Saranac River's Lower State Locks just west of Turtle Island.

To reach the trailhead from Lake Placid is a short ride. Find Averyville Road on the east end of town, just two blocks south—downhill—of the intersection (and traffic light) of NY 86 and NY 73. Turn southeast here (left if you're heading north, into town) onto Averyville Road, leaving the Lake Placid Municipal Park and mill pond to your right. At just under a mile you'll cross CR 35, or Old Military Road. Here there are signs for the Northville–Lake Placid Trail, a hiker's trunk trail that goes 132.2 miles to Northville. Set your car odometer to zero here, and proceed, crossing a bridge at the hiker's trailhead at 1.2 miles. Keep going, and at 3.7 miles you'll hit a dirt road. Pass through some fields. The road winds through a wood, and you bear left at a Y at 4.0 miles. Park anywhere you can in the unimproved, unmarked (legal) parking area. Security is sometimes an issue at trailheads—don't leave anything of value in your car if you can help it (like your notebook computer). Equip yourself for a serious outing, and prepare yourself. Bring water!

The trail from your ingress point at the top of Averyville Road may prove to be muddy and rocky in spots, which isn't helped by the fact that this is an old county road that still gets a bit of 4x4 traffic, most of it from hunters who keep seasonal camps along the route. You may meet some of them, splitting wood in midsummer in anticipation of hunting season, when dry wood is a prerequisite for comfortable camping. The road has been improved recently, and more surface improvement is planned. State funds are limited, however, so the measures that are taken won't significantly change the wilderness character of the road, nor will surface improvement (grading) proceed beyond the wetland areas of East Branch and Cold Brook.

0.0 Start pumping uphill.

You'll see snowmobile markers on the trees. The surface is excellent, sandy gravel. Head downhill, where the road is often washed out. Watch the ruts!

1.3 At a Y, bear right.

On the left is a dead-end trail that leads only a short distance. No bikes are allowed. You now have several miles of excellent, fast, bumpy riding ahead of you. In some places you can cruise at 14 mph, while at others you'll creep along at 5 mph. You won't need to dismount much—if at all—until reaching a few muddy swales around the 5-mile mark.

5.4 You arrive at Cold Brook—a wild, lively creek that flows in from the northern slopes of the Sawtooth Range.

This looks like the best place in the world to fish for trout, and I eagerly planned to do so—until I met a hunter on the road who lamented my plans apologetically. "Agh," he said, "they fish the livin' hell outta that pore little crik. I doubt there's anything alive in it still." That put an end to *that* wilderness dream. (Then I got suspicious—maybe he wanted the place all to himself!)

You're coming around the bend now, turning north, with the "crik" running north with you, on your left.

The Adirondack High Peaks

What a spot! Now you get some fine pine-woods singletrack riding. There are many places to pull over here and look at the deep, alluring pools, and opportunities for camping abound.

5.6 *A couple of footpaths will take you closer (presumably) to the creek after you pull uphill and away from it.*

There are some rocks here, but they end quickly. Finally, Cold Brook runs away to the northeast to join Flag Brook, and together they spill into the Saranac River and on to Lake Champlain.

6.7 *You'll start getting glimpses of the pond.*

You ride over the forgiving trail through hemlock-shrouded forests dotted with huge white pines and young birches.

6.8 *Pass a little unmarked trail on your left here.*

You might want to run down and take a look at the campsite that sits above the lake here, which is extra-attractive, or you may want to shortcut the tour by bringing your bike in this way. I recommend continuing.

7.0 At a T, go left. (This is a wilderness area, so technically, you've got to walk your bike or lock it up here.)

The right fork goes out to the canoe carry on Oseetah Lake. Follow the same great singletrack trail, only it's improving now.

7.2 Arrive at the sandy shore and wilderness beach area of Pine Pond.

You can get a little extra mileage by following the lakeshore, where the map shows a foot trail (canoe carry) heading for the Saranac River. This trail dies out soon, though. Lingering on at Pine Pond, I was witness to a hatch of mayflies and the little dimples of hundreds of rising trout. As for metaphors: "The creek may be fished out, but the pond is deep."

7.2 Unless you've done some creative planning, there's no way out of here other than the way you came in.

This is a long tour for some, and you may find yourself wishing you'd planned for a pull-out by boat, especially since you're facing a (rather wimpy) 400-foot total elevation gain on the way out. This sort of thing is possible, but it's a long way from the public boat access to the Pine Pond carry for someone who has to row or paddle: 4 miles round-trip, approximately, from the Second Pond campground headquarters on NY 3, and farther from the Saranac Lake (Lake Flower) public access on NY 86. I'd think seriously about the wisdom of putting a bike in a canoe, too, although this can easily be done by expert canoers who don't feel that wearing life preservers is beneath them (my advice is to tie the bike in). But if you're vacationing with a small trailerable fishing boat with a motor, that's the one-way ticket! Obviously, one poor soul will have to forfeit the ride to come and get you. Not quite needless to say, that person should also have the requisite map-reading and boat-handling skills to reach the canoe carry. (Time your pickup with deference to the blackflies. You may not want to wait around.)

Geologically, Pine Pond is a kettle hole. A large hunk of ice remained after the retreat of a glacier, gouging a neat hole in the sand, and the hole filled with water. Henry Thoreau's Walden Pond is also a kettle hole.

This tour is currently touted in the Essex County publication,

Mountain Bike Trails in the Adirondack Mountains of Essex County, New York, printed and distributed free of charge by the Essex County Visitor's Bureau. Included in this handy and well-done pamphlet are several other tours, most of them too short for including in this guidebook, but many meriting your exploration if you're in the area looking for more rides. It also includes a long list of town roads in the county that are suitable for mountain biking, based on the criteria of a dirt or gravel surface, light motor-vehicle traffic, a rural setting, and public right-of-way.

Camping Permits and General Information

Forest Ranger Headquarters: NYSDEC, Route 86, Box 296, Ray Brook, NY 12977-0296: 518-897-1200

Essex County Visitor's Bureau, Olympic Center, Lake Placid, NY 12946: 518-523-2445; Web site: http://www.lakeplacid.com

Bike Shops

High Peaks Cyclery, 331 Main Street, Lake Placid, NY: 518-523-3764; Web site: www.hpmac.com

Placid Planet Bicycles, 200 Saranac Ave., Lake Placid, NY: 518-523-4128

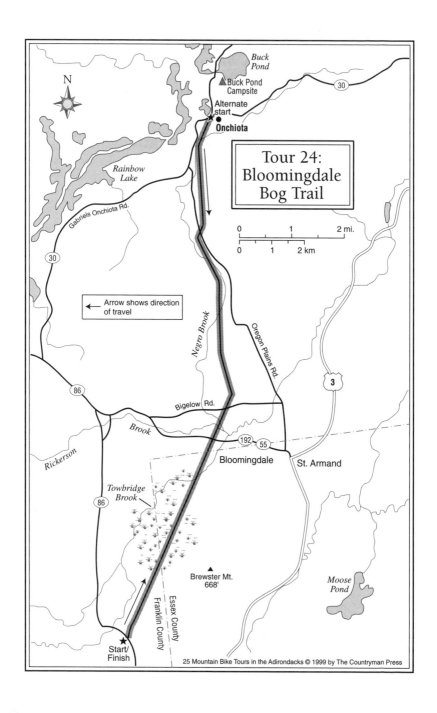

N

Buck
Pond

▲ Buck Pond
Campsite

Alternate
start

● Onchiota

Rainbow
Lake

Gabriels Onchiota Rd.

Tour 24:
Bloomingdale
Bog Trail

| 0 | | 1 | | 2 mi. |

| 0 | 1 | | 2 km |

30

← Arrow shows direction
of travel

Negro Brook

Oregon Plains Rd.

3

86

Bigelow Rd.

Brook

192 55

Rickerson

Bloomingdale   St. Armand

Towbridge
Brook

86

Brewster Mt.
668'

Moose
Pond

Essex County
Franklin County

Start/
Finish

25 Mountain Bike Tours in the Adirondacks © 1999 by The Countryman Press

24
Bloomingdale Bog Trail

Location: *Franklin and Essex Counties, Township of Harrietstown;
access from Saranac Lake or Buck Pond State Campsite and Public
Day-Use Area*
Terrain: *Flat*
Distance: *10 miles one-way*
Surface Conditions: *Hard sand, dirt, gravel, and some roots and
bumps*
Rating: *Beginner*
Maps: *Adirondack Canoe Map (cuts off last mile on north end); USGS:
Saranac Lake, Bloomingdale; a Franklin County map is recommended*
Highlights: *Extremely scenic, easy rail-trail ride with direct ingress from
Buck Pond State Campsite*

This popular trail is perhaps the flattest and most scenic ride in the
Adirondack Park. It's not likely to be so easy if you go the round trip of
20 miles, but such a ride is well within the reach of any avid and enthu-
siastic cyclist who has a few hours to spare. The nice part about this tour
is that you can turn around anywhere you like and still get the flavor of
the bog. Nor are you likely to run into a great many other riders, in spite
of the trail's growing popularity due to its presence in regional and local
promotional materials. This is state forest preserve—and miles of it.
Come prepared for any eventuality with first-aid kits, water, food, repair
tools, the works.

Because of the limited parking space at the southernmost access
in Saranac Lake, families especially will feel better about staging their
trip at the northern end of the trail, out of Buck Pond State Campsite
in Onchiota, where there's a day-use area, bathrooms, and tent sites.
From there, you roll right out of the campsite entrance and onto the

Bloomingdale Bog Trail. The more centrally located southern access (which crosses the bog area sooner, creating a stronger argument for beginning there if you can only go part way) can be found easily just 1.2 miles north of Saranac Lake off NY 86. Just watch carefully to your right as you come down a hill, after passing the Adirondack Medical Center on the right. Just before you cross a bog, a paved road appears on the right. Take it! This road turns almost immediately to dirt. Bear to the left into the parking area. A beaver pond is here at this time, and the trail sets out next to it.

To begin at the state campsite, first find your way to Onchiota, which you reach on CR 30 out of Gabriels (and then through Rainbow Lake), which is located north of Saranac Lake on NY 86. Turn right at "Gabe's" and go to "Onchae" that way, or go up NY 3 from Saranac Lake, through Bloomingdale. It's about a 25-minute ride either way.

Going through Gabriels, however, will enable you to see the southerly access first. Assuming you're a day tripper (and maybe you have a one-way driver, too), unload here and get on the rail trail straightaway. Coming back on the road, should you entertain such folly, is impractical and unproductive—NY 86 is a terrible ride, and NY 3 isn't much better, although it is preferable.

South to North

0.0 *Start out in the parking area amid the cherry tree saplings and the scattered splotches of milkweed, wildflowers, and tipping tendrils of quaking aspen.*

There are tamarack trees, too, those deciduous conifers that everyone thinks are dead come winter. The treadway is sometimes reduced from a doubletrack to a thin spaghetti strap down the middle, warm testimony to the trail's popularity with the fat-tire crowd. Soon you come to open areas rife with cawing ravens and a blue heron or two arcing noisily among the low hills and boggy plains. You get distant views of mountains and bog, punctuated by dark, isolated stands of black spruce. One mile to your right is Brewster Mountain and its associated ridges, and 5 miles to the north you are greeted with the winsome visage, rising like tropical islands out of the misty wetlands, of Negro, Blue, and James Hills.

2.0 Now you are smack in the middle of the great bog.

The only usable landmark is your odometer, unless you want to get fancy and triangulate your position using your orienteering compass—something that's always fun to do if the bugs aren't biting. But why bother on a straight track? You can't get lost because there's nowhere else to go.

By now you will have realized that you are in a very special place, indeed. Both the variety as well as the sheer biomass present is overwhelming, to the point that Mike Kudish, that legendary botanist of the forest preserve, declares it his "favorite place to botanize." There are plants here that appear nowhere else in the park.

2.9 Cross Twobridge Brook on a plank bridge, where the bridge-crossing sign has been well-peppered with shotgun pellets.

Don't worry, though. This kind of vandalism is normally restricted to hunting season. Now the railbed is sandy, quiet, and far removed from civilization. Profuse wildflowers within significant patches of reindeer moss follow. Pass under a power line.

3.8 Cross CR 55 (also shown on maps as NY 192), and keep going.

4.0 Cross two creeks within a short distance of each other, Rickerson Brook first, followed by Negro Brook.

At each of these bridges are views, one of a thousand feet of bog and another, to the right, of Whiteface Mountain (elevation 4,868'), some 15 miles to the east.

4.2 Cross Bigelow Road.

To the left a sign says BRIDGE CLOSED AT THIS TIME. To your right the road leads to Vermontville, and to the left is Negro Brook. Several unidentified dirt trails and tracks depart from this general area for places unknown. As you continue, the trail becomes drier, passing through more porous soils within a red-pine plantation. The trail is now sandier, glacial till.

5.5 Cross Negro Brook again as it meanders through a flat plain.

6.2 Cross Merrill Road (dirt).

Substantial all-terrain vehicle damage has occurred here, both to the trail and possibly the surrounding vegetation. Some trash can be seen lying around, but the trail continues to be attractive, wild, and greener as it penetrates a dense Scotch-pine forest that is over-stocked and badly in need of thinning to achieve its maximum, disease-free growth potential.

7.8 *Cross paved Oregon Plains Road, and keep going.*

8.5 *Cross an unidentified dirt road.*

9.4 *Cross Negro Brook yet again.*

You can hear and perhaps see CR 30 from this point.

9.8 *Cross CR 30, and ahead of you is the main entrance of Buck Pond State Campsite and Public Day-Use Area.*

10.0 *Enter the campground.*

Boating, canoeing (motors are not permitted in Buck Pond, but they are allowed in adjoining Lake Kushaqua), hiking, fishing, cycling, and, of course, camping, lying about, reading, walking, and other common leisurely pursuits are popular at Buck Pond. The Fulton Chain canoe route is accessible from here, given a portage of 0.75 mile between Rainbow Lake and Jones Pond, then down the outlet to Osgood Pond and Paul Smiths, and into the Seven Carries to the Saranacs (if you have a heavy canoe, you'll want wheels for that sized portage). At Buck Pond, ask for the publication *Canoe Franklin County,* which details this and similar tours by small boat.

Bloomingdale Bog is worth building a cycling weekend around, using either Buck Pond or the water-accessible state campsite at Lower Saranac Lake. It's also close enough to Meacham Lake State Campground as well as Fish Creek/Rollins Pond Public Campgrounds to stage day trips. Several loops and other creative approaches to the bog trail are possible using Oregon Plains Road, but to make your tour worthwhile, you've got to see the entire "Great Bog" from end to end.

Return the way you came, or settle in at the campsite and ride again tomorrow.

Camping Permits and General Information

Forest Ranger Headquarters: NYSDEC, Route 86, Box 296, Ray Brook, NY 12977-0296; 518-897-1200

Bike Shops

Barkeater Bike Shop, 49 Main Street, Saranac Lake, NY: 518-891-5207; 1-800-254-5207

World Cup Ski, Board, and Bike, 68 Park Street, Tupper Lake, NY: 518-359-9481; e-mail: worldcup@tvenet.com

25
Stony Creek Ponds and Indian Carry

Location: *Franklin County, Town of Harrietstown, Saranac Lakes Wild Forest*

Distance: *11.2 miles with 2-mile spur*

Terrain: *Flat to slightly hilly*

Surface Conditions: *Dirt roads*

Rating: *Beginner*

Maps: *Adirondack Canoe Map; The Adirondacks: High Peaks Region; The Adirondacks: Northwest Lakes; USGS: Stony Creek Mountain*

Highlights: *Scenic dirt roads in a peaceful setting with proximity to Fish Creek Pond/Rollins Pond Public Campgrounds*

This short "picnic" tour is a perfect ride for beginners—or just an easy half-day outing for anyone who wants a chance to relax or find a place to write, read, or draw beneath the big pines at Axton Landing. An added feature to the Stony Creek ride (which is south of NY 30/NY 3) is the dirt road to Upper Saranac Lake (north of NY 30/NY 3), where you can lock up your bikes and hike out to a nearby scenic point for a swim. Connecting this latter short spur to the tour requires a very short ride along the wide-shouldered highway. Frequent foot traffic is not unusual here, as this is the famed Indian Carry for canoeists crossing from the Raquette River to the Saranacs. A new carry was built off the northern-most bay of Second Pond several years ago, but many paddlers still opt to take the long way around to Upper Saranac by using Stony Creek Ponds Landing. Most of them either have rides, Kevlar boats, or wheels for their canoes. This has traditionally been a dreaded carry for those finishing up a rough week or two on the Fulton Chain (it's a lot easier to portage a bike).

Indian Carry and Corey's Road are located roughly between Tupper

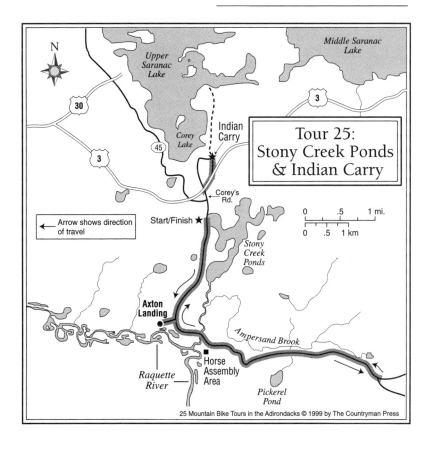

N

Upper
Saranac
Lake

Middle Saranac
Lake

30

3

Indian
Carry

Corey
Lake

45

3

Tour 25:
Stony Creek Ponds
& Indian Carry

Corey's
Rd.

0   .5   1 mi.

0   .5   1 km

← Arrow shows direction
of travel

Start/Finish ★

Stony
Creek
Ponds

Axton
Landing

Ampersand Brook

Horse
Assembly
Area

Raquette
River

Pickerel
Pond

25 Mountain Bike Tours in the Adirondacks © 1999 by The Countryman Press

and Saranac Lakes, just 0.5 mile east of the intersection (on the north side of NY 3) of CR 45, another scenic though paved and hilly road that follows the western shore of Upper Saranac Lake. From the junction of NY 30/NY 3, a few miles east of Tupper Lake, follow NY 3 toward Saranac Lake. Indian Carry will be on your left at 2.4 miles, and Corey's Road is just before it on your right at 2.3 miles. Indian Carry is 13 miles west of the town of Saranac Lake, in which case Corey's Road will be on your left, 0.1 mile beyond it. Turn in where you see signs for the Cold River Ranch. That's Corey's Road, a.k.a. Ampersand Road. You can inquire at the ranch about horseback riding into the Cold River Region of the High Peaks Wilderness Area, which is a very interesting trip for those so inclined. Follow Corey's Road 0.3 mile until you reach Stony Creek

Ponds Landing, and park (this is where canoeists put their boats in the water). There are several places to park near the landing, so look around if things are busy. Set your cyclometer to zero, and bike south.

0.0 This section of road is paved.

> Good views of Third Pond on your left are followed by forests and seasonal camps.

0.2 Pass a wetland area on your right.

0.9 The road turns to dirt.

1.0 Tall, skinny red pines appear in a thick forest atmosphere.

1.6 Turn right onto the Axton Landing Road.

> The landing is actually a shallow beach that enters the Raquette River through a small backwater. Many people use this area for short-term camping, and canoe groups from all over the country have been known to stage trips from this location, which to me, together with places like Trombleys Landing, embodies the true flavor of the north woods. (Trombleys can also be biked. The trailhead begins on the south side of the NY 30/NY 3 intersection discussed earlier. It's just under a 4-mile intermediate trip.) You can camp here or just sit and watch the river flow. Upper Saranac Lake is a much better place to swim, however. Continue around the loop to follow the dirt road out.

1.9 Turn right onto Corey's Road again.

2.4 Cross the bridge at the very scenic creek between First and Second Pond.

> These are the Stony Creek Ponds. There are primitive campsites here on the bridge's east side, and at least a few campers will be around. Part of the reason for the area's popularity is the Stony Creek Horse Assembly Area for equestrians traveling to Raquette Falls and beyond, which you'll see a little farther down the road. You can park here, also, but you can't bike the alluring dirt road you'll see heading into the wilderness area.
>
> The road climbs.

3.7 Pass the trailhead for Pickerel Pond on your right.

4.0 Pass an unmarked road on your right.

The footbridge on Upper Saranac Lake

5.2 Cross a small, attractive wetland area along Ampersand Brook, leaving another dirt road to your left.

There are limited views here.

5.6 On your right is the Seward Mountain Trailhead parking lot for the High Peaks Wilderness Area.

This is your advised turn-around point, since another 0.4 mile beyond here the road is gated private property. Consider hiding or locking your bike at the trailhead area and stretching your legs with a short walk into the wilderness in another direction. Then head out, and go for Indian Carry if you're still game.

5.6 Go back past the Stony Creek Ponds Landing, and out to NY 3 (you can also drive over). Turn right, exercising caution, until you reach the carry road (dirt) at 0.1 mile, where you turn left.

Indian Carry is less than a mile long, and the payoff is big. Aside from the scenery and a good, close look at the lake from the water's edge, try to make the time for the short hike over the footbridge and out to the point, where camping is permitted. And if you have a canoe, better yet. You can launch it here and head for one of the lake's many campsites. But get an early start, and be careful. This is a big lake, and conditions can sometimes be treacherous.

Return the way you came.

Camping Permits and General Information

Forest Ranger Headquarters: NYSDEC, Route 86, Box 296, Ray Brook, NY 12977-0296: 518-897-1200

Bike Shops

Barkeater Bike Shop, 49 Main Street, Saranac Lake, NY: 518-891-5207; 1-800-254-5207

World Cup Ski, Board, and Bike, 68 Park Street, Tupper Lake, NY: 518-359-9481; e-mail: worldcup@tvenet.com

Forest Preserve Information

NYSDEC Regional Offices
Northwestern Adirondacks
NYSDEC
6739 US Highway 11
Potsdam, NY 13676
315-265-3090

Western Adirondacks
NYSDEC
Route 812
Lowville, NY 13367
315-376-3521

Southwestern Adirondacks
NYSDEC
225 North Main Street
Herkimer, NY 13350
315-866-6330

Northern and Central Adirondacks
NYSDEC
Route 86, Box 296
Ray Brook, NY 12977-0296
518-897-1200

Eastern Adirondacks
NYSDEC
Hudson Street Extension, Box 220
Warrensburg, NY 12885
518-668-5441

Southern Adirondacks
NYSDEC
701 South Main Street
Box 458
Northville, NY 12134
518-863-4545

Adirondack Organizations

Adirondack Mountain Bike Association
c/o Ted Christodaro
PO Box 390
Inlet, NY 13360
315-357-3281

Adirondack Region Bike Club
331 Main Street
Lake Placid, NY 12946
518-891-1780
www.northnet.org/gemboy/arbc.html

Adirondack North Country Association
183 Broadway
Saranac Lake, NY 12983
518-891-6200
Web site: www.adirondack.org
e-mail: anca@northnet.org
Publishes *Bikeways of the Adirondack North Country,* a biking map.

Adirondack Mountain Club
814 Goggins Road
Lake George, NY 12845
1-800-395-8080
Web site: www.adk.org

Bicycling Advocacy Groups

Rails to Trails Conservancy
1400 16th St. NW, Suite 300
Washington, DC 20036

NORBA (National Off-Road Bicycle Association)
1 Olympic Plaza
Colorado Springs, CO 80909

Adventure Cycling Association
150 E. Pine Street
PO Box 8308
Missoula, MT 59807-8308
1-800-721-8719
Expeditions, maps, technical/nutritional advice, advocacy.

Craig Wolf
Bike to Work Resource Guide
Chicago DOT
121 N. LaSalle St., Room 406
Chicago, IL 60602

New York Bicycling Coalition
PO Box 7335
Albany, NY 12224

Bike-Up America
Box 116
826 Proctor Ave.
Ogdensburg, NY 13669

Biking Is Kind to the Environment (B.I.K.E.)
Box 667
Chatham, NJ 07928

Pedals For Progress
86 East Main St.
High Bridge, NJ 08829
This organization reconditions bikes to send to South America.
   Newsletter.

International Mountain Bicycling Organization (IMBA)
Box 7578
Boulder, CO 80306

League of American Wheelmen
The National Organization of Bicyclists
190 W. Ostend St., Suite 120
Baltimore, MD 21230-3731

Bicycle Federation of America
1506 21st St. NW, Suite 200
Washington, DC 20036-1008
Various pamphlets available.

Women's Mountain Bike and Tea Society (WOMBATS)
PO Box 757
Fairfax, CA 94978
24-Hour Hotline: 415-459-0980
FAX: 415-459-0832
Advocacy, workshops, newsletters, national chapters, events.

Let Backcountry Guides Take You There

Our experienced backcountry authors will lead you to the finest trails, parks, and back roads in the following areas:

50 Hikes Series

50 Hikes in the Maine Mountains
50 Hikes in Southern and Coastal Maine
50 Hikes in Vermont
50 Hikes in the White Mountains
50 More Hikes in New Hampshire
50 Hikes in Connecticut
50 Hikes in Massachusetts
50 Hikes in the Hudson Valley
50 Hikes in the Adirondacks
50 Hikes in Central New York
50 Hikes in Western New York
50 Hikes in New Jersey
50 Hikes in Eastern Pennsylvania
50 Hikes in Central Pennsylvania
50 Hikes in Western Pennsylvania
50 Hikes in the Mountains of North
    Carolina
50 Hikes in Northern Virginia
50 Hikes in Ohio
50 Hikes in Michigan

Walks and Rambles Series

Walks and Rambles on Cape Cod and
    the Islands
Walks and Rambles in Rhode Island
More Walks and Rambles in Rhode
    Island
Walks and Rambles on the Delmarva
    Peninsula
Walks and Rambles in Southwestern
    Ohio
Walks and Rambles in Ohio's Western
    Reserve
Walks and Rambles in the Western
    Hudson Valley
Walks and Rambles on Long Island

25 Bicycle Tours Series

25 Bicycle Tours in Maine
30 Bicycle Tours in New Hampshire
25 Bicycle Tours in Vermont
25 Mountain Bike Tours in Vermont
25 Bicycle Tours on Cape Cod and the
    Islands
25 Mountain Bike Tours in
    Massachusetts
30 Bicycle Tours in New Jersey
25 Mountain Bike Tours in New Jersey
25 Bicycle Tours in the Adirondacks
25 Mountain Bike Tours in the
    Adirondacks
30 Bicycle Tours in the Finger Lakes
    Region
25 Bicycle Tours in the Hudson Valley
25 Bicycle Tours in the Twin Cities and
    Southeastern Minnesota
30 Bicycle Tours in Wisconsin
25 Mountain Bike Tours in the
    Hudson Valley
25 Bicycle Tours in Ohio's
    Western Reserve
25 Bicycle Tours in Maryland
25 Bicycle Tours on Delmarva
25 Bicycle Tours in and around
    Washington, D.C.
25 Bicycle Tours in Coastal Georgia and
    the Carolina Low Country
25 Bicycle Tours in the Texas Hill Country
    and West Texas

We offer many more books on hiking, fly-fishing, travel, nature, and other subjects, available at bookstores and outdoor stores everywhere. For a free catalog, call 1-800-245-4151 or write to us at The Countryman Press, PO Box 748, Woodstock, Vermont 05091. You can find us on the web at www.countrymanpress.com